Creative Resources
for
Bulletin Boards

Creative Resources for
Bulletin Boards
in the
Early
Childhood
Classroom

Judy Herr
and Yvonne Libby

Bulletin board and pattern drawings by Yvonne Libby
Text Illustrations by Joan Waites

gryphon house
Beltsville, Maryland

Acknowledgments

During the years between our first conceptualization of this book and the book's completion, there were many individuals whose creative ideas, support and encouragement helped us. Our sincere thanks to all of them.

First, to our parents who fostered our creativity and love of young children.

To our typist, Vicki Weber, who so ably transcribed our writing and ideas.

To our colleagues in early childhood education whom we have worked with at the University of Wisconsin-Stout.

To all students majoring in early childhood education at the University of Wisconsin-Stout and the children enrolled in the Child and Family Study Center who have enjoyed the bulletin board ideas presented in this book.

Finally, to the students majoring in early childhood and the professionals who use *Creative Resources for the Early Childhood Classroom* and encouraged us to share additional bulletin board ideas.

Copyright © 1997 Judy Herr and Yvonne Libby
Published by Gryphon House, Inc.
10726 Tucker Street, Beltsville, MD 20705
www.ghbooks.com

Printed in the United States of America.

Text Illustrations: Joan Waites
Bulletin board and pattern drawings by: Yvonne Libby

Library of Congress Cataloging-in-Publication Data

Herr, Judy.
        Creative resources for bulletin boards in the early childhood classroom / Judy Herr and Yvonne Libby; bulletin board and pattern drawings by Yvonne Libby, text illustrations by Joan Waites.
            p. cm.
        Includes index.
    ISBN 0-87659-183-7
    1. Bulletin boards--United States--Handbooks, manuals, etc. 2. Early childhood education--Activity programs--United States--Handbooks, manuals, etc.   I. Libby, Yvonne.   II. Title.
    LB1043.58.H47 1997   96-42036

Table of Contents

Patterns for Letters and Numerals

Introduction

Bulletin boards are essential in the early childhood classroom. Boards created for children are important tools for:

    introducing new concepts and clarifying existing ones,

    stimulating language development,

    encouraging discussion,

    sharing events that will or have happened and

    adding aesthetic appeal to the environment.

Bulletin boards are a vital tool for communicating what is happening in the classroom and for sharing notices and announcements with parents, staff, visitors and volunteers. Bulletin boards also add color, decoration and interest to the classroom.

The most effective classroom bulletin boards involve the children. They encourage the children to manipulate pieces of the board. Consequently, these boards are called interactive bulletin boards. By interacting with the bulletin board materials, children can learn a variety of concepts, such as size, number, shape and color, and develop important skills. These skills include visual discrimination, eye-hand coordination, one-to-one correspondence, decoding, numeral recognition, symbol recognition and language skills.

In addition to interactive bulletin boards, there are three other types of bulletin boards that can be used effectively with children in early childhood programs. These are referred to as child-created, decorative and conceptual. Although the bulletin boards are designated as being in one of the four categories, the categories overlap. For example, any type of bulletin board could aesthetically enhance the learning environment and, therefore, be called decorative. Similarly, every bulletin board could help promote concept and language development and be categorized as conceptual.

The purpose for writing *Creative Resources for Bulletin Boards in the Early Childhood Classroom* is to help you prepare bulletin boards that will be appealing to young children, hold their attention and help them learn concepts and skills.

The first section of the book, How to Create Effective Bulletin Boards, includes information on the four types of bulletin boards and describes how to prepare effective bulletin boards. Information on the use of color, types of coloring media, preserving materials and criteria for evaluating bulletin boards is included. In addition, you will learn how to choose and prepare background materials, borders and lettering.

The second section of the book contains fifty examples of bulletin boards. For each bulletin board there is an illustration, a list of related curriculum themes, alternate titles, a list of materials needed to prepare the bulletin board, directions for preparing the bulletin board, how to vary the basic bulletin board idea and a list of developmental goals including skills that children develop by interacting with the bulletin board.

The third section of this book contains examples of classroom labels, name tags and cubby tags. The fourth section of the book contains letters and numerals that can be used to make captions on bulletin boards or teacher-made materials, such as charts and games.

The illustrations and patterns in this book can be used for purposes other than creating bulletin boards, such as:
preparing charts,
labeling areas and materials,
creating large story board characters,
making puppets,
preparing flannel board pieces,
creating teacher-made games and
developing transparencies for storytelling.

How to Create Effective Bulletin Boards

Types of Bulletin Boards

Each type of bulletin board has a purpose. Child-created bulletin boards are used by early child-hood professionals for displaying children's work. Art projects, writing samples and photographs are examples of materials that may be displayed. Children take pride in contributing to a child-created bulletin board. Classroom visitors and parents also enjoy viewing this type of visual display showcasing the children's activities.

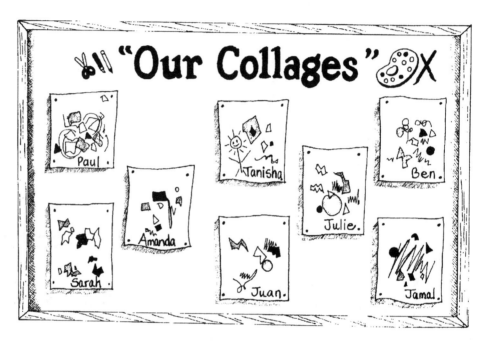

Decorative bulletin boards are used for aesthetically enhancing the classroom learning environment. Generally, teachers are noted for creating or purchasing commercially prepared materials for this type of bulletin board. Examples of decorative bulletin boards include Welcome to School, Valentine's Day, Thanksgiving and Spring bulletin boards.

Conceptual bulletin boards are designed to pictorialize concepts. For example, to represent plant life the board would include the stages of plant growth, beginning with a seed and proceeding with the development of roots, stem and leaves. This visual representation helps young children understand the concept.

Interactive bulletin boards are designed with materials that can be manipulated by children. They are the most stimulating type of bulletin board and maintain children's attention. Frequently interactive bulletin boards are described as "hands-on." Developmentally appropriate bulletin boards enhance various skills of young children. In addition to aesthetic appreciation and concept formation, this instructional medium promotes the development of an appreciation for the printed word, eye-hand coordination skills, visual discrimination skills, left-to-right progression skills, one-to-one correspondence skills, problem-solving skills, letter recognition, numeral recognition, color recognition and small muscle coordination skills.

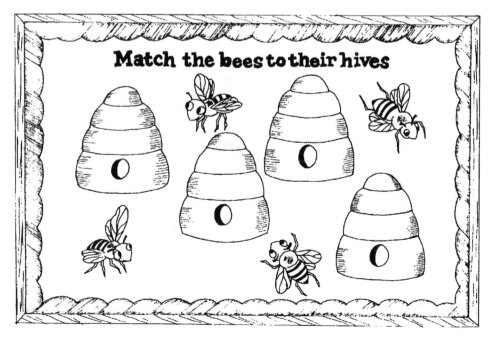

Match the bees to their hives

Principles for Constructing Bulletin Boards

Creating effective bulletin boards requires the following key principles. Always keep the bulletin board simple so that its organization appears clear. A cluttered bulletin board can be confusing to young children as well as adults. To hold the attention of the viewer, avoid crowding material. Focus the viewer's attention by using a few simple figures. Surround the figures with ample open space that will assist the viewers in focusing their attention. It is also important to note that a balanced arrangement of bulletin board figures will hold children's interest. Study the examples provided in this book. They are examples of bulletin boards that will be appealing to young children.

Since young children are in the process of developing concepts about their world, figures should always be in proportion to each other. For example, a chicken should be smaller than a pig. A hamster should be smaller than a puppy. A horse should be larger than a lamb. Moreover, body parts should be in proportion to the human figure.

Color is the key to creating effective bulletin boards. Therefore it is always important to exercise care when selecting coloring tools. When bulletin board pieces need the application of color, there are several different types of media that can be successfully applied. Experienced teachers report that craypas and watercolor markers are the most effective, although crayons can be an interesting medium. However, the finished appearance of the craypas and watercolor markers are preferred by most teachers over the crayons. Craypas and watercolor markers are easier to apply, projecting a polished professional appearance.

Craypas—Craypas are coloring tools that are oil-based. They can be purchased at art supply stores and through school supply catalogs. Craypas usually produce a smoother appearance if correctly applied. Many early childhood teachers feel more confident applying colors using craypas than crayons.

The most effective method of applying color with craypas is by making a horizontal sweeping motion. To do this, begin by removing the individual paper wrapper that identifies the color. Then place your thumb and forefinger on the center of the coloring tool. By holding the craypa in this position, you can apply uniform pressure on the surface of the material. You will discover that this technique produces a more even distribution of color. After applying color with a craypa, use a paper tissue to evenly distribute the color. To prevent mixing colors, use a separate piece of tissue for each color that you smooth.

Watercolor Felt-Tip Markers—Watercolor felt-tip markers can be purchased at most retail stores that carry school or stationery supplies. The most effective markers are those with a wide felt-tip. To apply the color evenly, begin by drawing vertical lines from the same direction. For example, begin by placing the marker on the upper left corner of the material to be colored. Draw a straight line down from the top of the material. When the line is completed, carefully remove the marker from the material. Then move the marker back to the top left corner of the material again. Carefully align the tip of the marker next to the first line. Position the marker to avoid an overlap of color or space between color. Then continue repeating this procedure until the entire surface of the material is covered with color. This procedure may take repeated practice to master.

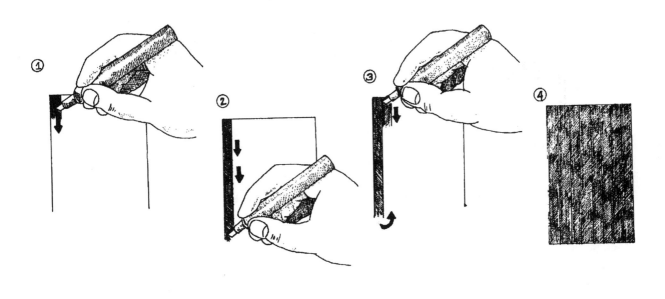

Preserving Materials

You will discover that almost every early childhood teacher's objective is to work smarter, not harder. One way to work smarter is to prepare durable figures that will last for several years. To do this, begin by selecting a grade of paper or tagboard that is appropriate for the age and abilities of your children. Remember that young children are better at grasping and handling a thicker grade of paper such as tagboard or cardboard. This type of paper is also more durable since it does not bend or crush easily with frequent use.

Once the materials have been prepared, ask yourself this question: "Will I have an opportunity to use any of the bulletin board figures or captions at another time?" You will probably find opportunities to reuse or redesign the original materials. Some teachers are skillful at interchanging bulletin board titles and figures from year to year. For example, they may reuse the same bulletin board letters for the caption HAPPY VALENTINE'S DAY next year, changing only the background paper and figures. There may be occasions when they use the entire bulletin board again the following year. In this case, it is important that teachers carefully preserve the figures.

One method of preserving bulletin board figures is to laminate them. Lamination is a process in which paper and tagboard are covered on both sides with a transparent plastic film and rolled through a machine while heat is applied to permanently seal the materials in the plastic film. If you do not have access to a laminating machine, purchase clear contact paper at a local discount or specialty store. It takes practice to successfully apply clear contact paper. Begin by collecting your figures and choosing a large, flat surface on which to work. Practice applying the clear contact paper to scrap pieces prior to key figures or captions. This may save you the time and effort of having to reproduce the figures if the contact paper on the finished product is not smooth.

Using a laminating machine is the fastest and easiest technique to obtain uniformity. As a result, many early childhood directors and school principals consider a laminating machine a necessity. They realize that by laminating, it is possible to prepare durable games, name tags, charts and bulletin board figures. This is a way of saving valuable preparation time as well as recycling materials, therefore, reducing expenditures for classroom materials. The machine and laminating film can be purchased through office and school supply stores.

Choosing Color

Simplicity is an important principle when selecting and focusing color. The stronger the color used, the more attention it gets. Color is an attention-grabber, so limit the number of main colors to two or three, including their tints and shades. A bulletin board with many colors is overstimulating. Simplicity in design and materials is also important. Choose only one type of background material and cover the entire board. Change the appearance of the board by using different background materials.

Background Materials

Aluminum foil	Burlap	Construction paper
Computer paper	Cork	Crepe paper
Doilies	Felt	Gift wrapping paper
Greeting cards	Maps	Newspapers, especially comics
Shelf paper	Tissue paper	Wallpaper

Holidays, such as Valentine's Day and St. Patrick's Day are associated with particular colors as are certain things, such as the sky, clouds, grass, water and animals. To facilitate concept development in young children, always select the associated color. For example, cows should not be colored pink or purple but should be as realistic as possible.

Basic terms you need to know about color are primary: colors, secondary colors, complementary colors and warm and cool colors. Reviewing and understanding these color concepts will help in planning and creating bulletin boards.

Primary Colors—Red, blue and yellow are the primary colors. The term "pure colors" is frequently used when describing these colors. Pure colors cannot be created by combining any other colors. Stop for a moment and think about comparing color to music. Primary colors are like the basic notes on the scale. However, listening to music and hearing only one note at a time would lack interest. To create variety, sharps, flats and chords need to be added. Similarly, when using color, you need to add variety.

Secondary Colors—By mixing equal parts of the primary colors, you will be creating secondary colors. For example, when you add equal parts of red and yellow, you create the color orange. Similarly, to create the color green add equal amounts of blue and yellow. By adding equal parts of red and blue you will create violet.

Complementary Colors—Complementary colors are those that are opposite each other on a color wheel. Consequently, they are not used in creating colors. For example, red complements green, blue complements orange and yellow complements violet.

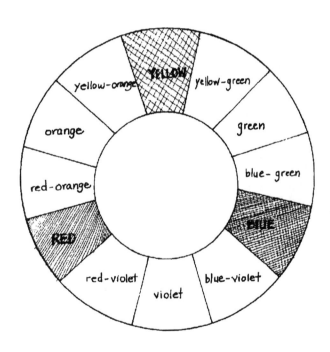

Warm vs. Cool Colors—The warm colors are red, yellow and orange. These colors remind us of the sun and fire. There are, however, degrees of warm colors. Examples include shades of red, yellow and orange. Violet, blue and dark green are cold colors. They remind us of leaves and water. As a result, they have the effect of making us feel cool. Shades and tints of these colors are especially important as a background material on bulletin boards.

Emotional Effect of Color—Color affects both adults and children in how they feel and act. The following chart explains the emotional affect of colors.

Emotional Affect of Colors

BLUE	Cooling
GREEN	Cooling
YELLOW	Stimulating
RED	Exciting and demands attention
VIOLET	Soothing
ORANGE	Stimulating
GRAY	Cold
BROWN	Restful and warming
WHITE	Cheerful

Recent research shows that color can affect feelings and behavior. For example, studies show people in blue light are more restful and less active. Unlike blue, red demands attention. Thus, use red sparsely in your classroom. Constructing an eye-catching title color or adding red accents or details to bulletin board outlines are two ways to use red effectively.

Personality type influences color preferences. Extroverts prefer the color red while introverts prefer blue. The color yellow, like red, demands attention. It is a cheery, stimulating and attention-drawing color. The color yellow is an effective choice for captions and borders on bulletin boards.

General Principles—When planning your bulletin board, remember that color should be used to emphasize key concepts. A general principle is the stronger the color, the more limited its use. Strong colors, sometimes called warm colors, advance. Use these colors for a caption or key outline. On the other hand, cool colors recede and are usually more effective as background colors. The most effective background colors to use on a bulletin board are pale and are called tints. When possible, choose colors that complement the existing classroom color scheme. Light colors and sometimes white can also be effectively used as background colors.

Borders

A border creates a frame for the bulletin board. Borders can be teacher-created or purchased through school supply stores or early childhood catalogs. Depending upon the bulletin board design, borders can be simple or complex. A general principle is that a bulletin board containing numerous figures should be framed with a simple border. There are five types of borders; strip, scalloped, reversed scalloped, zigzag and chain.

Strip Border

Cut strips from construction paper, wrapping paper, magazine pictures, tagboard, crepe paper, fabric, the newspaper, ribbons, cardboard, cork or corrugated paper to prepare this type of border.

Scalloped Border

Construct the scalloped border by tracing half way around a saucer or coffee lid using a soft lead pencil. Using a sharp cutting tool, cut the border from the material. To create a different look, reverse the design.

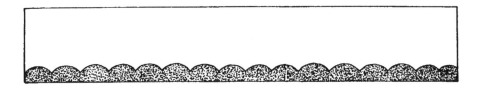

Reversed Scalloped Border

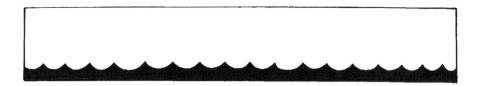

Zigzag Border

Create a zigzag border by first cutting a large strip from construction paper, wrapping paper or any other material, such as those suggested in the strip border. Cut a pattern of repeated triangles as illustrated.

Chain Border

Make a chain border by cutting strips of paper and stapling or pasting them together. Generally teachers prefer stapling or gluing because it provides more durable results.

Bulletin Board Captions

To make interesting and effective captions or titles, use primary colors that complement the border and outlines. When should captions be constructed with upper case or capital letters? This depends upon the title and teacher preference. If the title consists of a complete sentence, the first letter of the sentence is capitalized. Then lower case letters are used for the remainder of the sentence. Punctuation also needs to be placed at the end of the sentence. When you are using phrases, capitalize the first letter of each word, except words, such as "and," "at," "in," "on" and "of." Listed below are examples of bulletin board phrases and sentences.

Phrase	Complete Sentence
Green Frog	See the green frog.
Magic Rabbits	Find the magic rabbits.
Firefighters' Hats	Match the firefighters' hats.
Dogs	Find the largest dog.

Letters

Preparing a set of letters and numerals to be used as stencils saves time. To do this, trace the letters and numerals in this book on heavyweight paper or tagboard. Then cut the letters out with sharp scissors or a razor. Store the letters and numerals in a convenient box, tray or file folder. When preparing bulletin board captions, trace these stencils on paper or fabric.

A title or caption usually conveys the dominant theme of the bulletin board. Consequently, the letters should be carefully prepared to project a professional image. Begin by choosing an effective color for attracting attention. Attention-getting letters can be cut from brochures, newspaper, wrapping paper, calendars and magazines. To add interest, letters can also be covered with aluminum foil, yarn, glitter or textured paint, or print titles using tempera paint, craypas or felt-tip markers. Whichever method is used, the letters should be in proportion to the size of the bulletin board figures and the bulletin board. It is also important that the lettering contrast with the background color(s) used on the bulletin board. For example, dark blue letters complement a light blue background.

Preparing Patterns

There are several successful methods for preparing patterns. Photocopying pages and increasing or decreasing the images to the preferred size is the easiest method. When pictures in a book are the desired size, cut or trace the pictures. To create temporary patterns, use tissue paper and a soft lead pencil. Lay the tissue paper over the desired piece, trace the outline(s) using the pencil. Using sharp scissors, cut the outline(s) from the tissue paper.

Study the bulletin boards and patterns in this book, then sketch the figures freehand, making modifications as desired. You can also use either an opaque or overhead projector to enlarge and trace the figures. As you proceed, remember that the bulletin boards illustrated in the book may be used in two ways. They can be used exactly as sketched in the book, or you may prefer to use the basic idea and design your own bulletin board. Bulletin boards begin on page 26 and patterns on page 128.

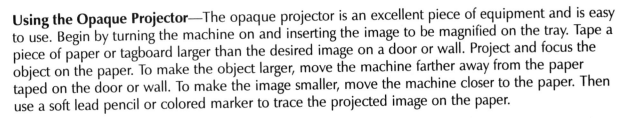

Using the Opaque Projector—The opaque projector is an excellent piece of equipment and is easy to use. Begin by turning the machine on and inserting the image to be magnified on the tray. Tape a piece of paper or tagboard larger than the desired image on a door or wall. Project and focus the object on the paper. To make the object larger, move the machine farther away from the paper taped on the door or wall. To make the image smaller, move the machine closer to the paper. Then use a soft lead pencil or colored marker to trace the projected image on the paper.

Using the Overhead Projector—Another useful tool for preparing bulletin boards is the overhead projector. Select a picture to be enlarged. It may be from familiar items, such as a storybook, greeting card or newspaper. Place a clear sheet of acetate on the picture. Trace around the image using a washable marker designed for transparencies, then project the image onto a wall and follow the same procedures as with the opaque projector.

Fastening Materials

Carefully consider safety when choosing fastening materials. In early childhood settings, stick pins or thumb tacks should be avoided. Instead use staples, rubber cement, velcro, bulletin board wax or putty. Note that rubber cement usually is effective only when using lightweight materials; however, bulletin board wax, putty, cup hooks or map pins are more effective for heavier materials.

Some teachers prefer to staple materials on the board. This method can be effective. However, sometimes the materials are damaged while removing the staples. This can be frustrating, especially if you are planning to reuse the materials.

Holders

Many interactive bulletin boards require pockets or containers to hold the individual pieces. Holders may be cardboard boxes, trays, pails, berry baskets, envelopes or resealable plastic bags. Select a container or pocket that will complement the general appearance of the board. When using a box or tray, try to complement the color of the bulletin board. Boxes can be covered with the same material as either the border or background materials, if desired.

The weight and number of materials should determine the type and size of the container used. Containers may be attached to or placed adjacent to the bulletin board. Some boxes or transparent bags can be stapled directly to the board. If containers are attached to the board, make sure that the box or tray does not protrude too far or the children may accidentally knock it off the board.

Placement of Bulletin Boards

Whenever possible, bulletin boards should be at the children's eye level. Since children vary in height, the placement of a bulletin board in early childhood classrooms can range from 28 to 45 inches from the floor. Place the bulletin board so that the middle of the board is at eye-level for the majority of children.

Storing Bulletin Boards

An effective bulletin board for young children takes time to plan, construct and post. As a result, many teachers choose to recycle their bulletin board figures, background materials and titles. To do this, the materials must be carefully stored. There are several successful methods for storing bulletin board materials. The most inexpensive method is to staple two pieces of tagboard together, creating a large envelope. Print the title of the board and date used on the upper right corner of the tagboard envelope. The bulletin board pieces should be carefully inserted into the envelope to avoid bending. Place the envelope on a flat, dry surface to avoid warping in humid conditions.

Two other storage strategies include cardboard artist envelopes and a large file cabinet with drawers. Although the file cabinet is convenient, it does require space and is expensive. Because of the expense and space requirement, this type of storage may not be feasible. You will find that the artist envelope is less expensive, portable and requires less storage space.

Evaluating Bulletin Boards

Evaluation is an integral part of improving your preparation of effective bulletin boards. Begin this process by applying the criteria listed below on the bulletin board evaluation check list. After you have finished, review the items checked in the needs improvement category. Ask yourself how you could improve the bulletin board. By evaluating the bulletin board, you will improve your skills in designing professional, appealing bulletin boards for the early childhood classroom.

Criteria	Acceptable	Needs Improvement
1. Is the purpose clear to the children, staff, parents and classroom visitors?		
2. Is the bulletin board placed at the children's eye-level?		
3. Does the bulletin board hold the children's attention?		
4. Does the bulletin board add to the children's knowledge and promote the development of skills?		
5. Does the bulletin board motivate action by stimulating the children's curiosity?		
6. Is the organization simple, clear and easily understood?		
7. Is the bulletin board designed with colors that harmonize?		
8. Does the background color complement the figures and lettering?		
9. Are the figures easily recognizable from a distance?		
10. Is the content of the board developmentally appropriate for the group of children?		
11. Are the title letters in proportion to the bulletin board size and figures?		
12. Are safe materials and attachments used?		
13. Does the board help children understand and appreciate different cultures? (if applicable)		
14. Does the board help the children appreciate differences and similarities? (If applicable)		

Making Name Tags

"Who is that child? Is it Tommy or Teddy?" These questions are echoed over and over again at the beginning of the school year and when new children are introduced. Parents also appreciate the use of name tags to help them identify their children's playmates. To assist staff members and volunteers in learning names and identifying children, construct simple name tags. Usually when there is not a high turnover of children, name tags are worn only at the beginning of the year, at special events, such as holiday parties with parents and on field trips.

Frequently, center or school staff prepare two sets of name tags. One set, containing the child's first name, is primarily for classroom use. Another set of name tags is used for the children to wear on field trips. Printed on these tags, in addition to the child's first name, is the name, address and telephone number of the center. This information may be useful if a child accidentally strays from the group. Also, the availability of the child's first name can be a useful tool for a tour director.

Taking attendance is another purpose for using name tags in early childhood settings. These tags can be kept on a bulletin board or in a basket at the entrance to a classroom. As children arrive, they put on their name tags. By reviewing the remaining tags, the teacher can easily determine who is absent.

Considerations—Consider the size of the name tag. Tags must be large enough so that the child's name can be easily seen from a distance. On the other hand, name tags can be too large. When this happens, the name tag can be cumbersome, interfering with the child's comfort and play.

Durability is also important. Select materials on the basis of durability. In addition, name tags can be planned to coordinate with curriculum themes. For example, during a unit on farm animals, name tags in the shape of a specific farm animal can be used.

Color needs to be considered when planning name tags. For example, using a light colored material for the name tag and a dark felt-tip marker is an effective combination.

Name tags can be worn either on the front or back of the body. Most teachers prefer the front of the body, allowing the child's name to be visible during group time. This is a particularly important aid for substitute teachers or classroom volunteers. Resource people, whether in the classroom or at field trip sites, also appreciate having the children wear name tags.

Traditionally, teachers have used a variety of methods to attach name tags. Shoestrings, yarn, thin rope, safety pins and masking tape have all been used. Name tag attachments, like curriculum, should be planned by considering the developmental level of the children. There are drawbacks to all types of name tag attachments. Children can put name tags that are attached to shoestrings, yarn or a thin piece of rope around their necks without adult assistance. However, when name tags are displayed by one of these methods, they can be easily pulled or twisted. This could cause a possible irritation or even injury. Safety pins are used in some centers. The drawback of using safety pins for attaching name tags is that adult assistance is required. Then, too, the child's clothing may be damaged by the safety pin. Masking tape is another option. While masking tape is probably the safest way to attach the name tag, it is not durable. Consequently, the tape may need to be replaced several times each day. It is also possible for the children to lose their name tags.

Name tags can be constructed from a variety of materials. Disposable commercially purchased name identification tags and name tags made from construction paper are the least durable. You may prefer using badges or buttons as name tags. Because of their durability, some teachers prefer felt, fabric, interfacing, leather, press board and wood materials to create name tags.

The materials selected for the name tags will determine the preparation process. A wood burning set can be used for engraving the child's name on leather or wood. Permanent felt-tip markers can be used on felt, fabric, interfacing paper and press board. After printing the child's name, a protective spray, such as Scotchguard® can be applied to repel dirt and other stains on fabric name tags.

You will note that the name tags included in this book complement most of the themes in *Creative Resources for the Early Childhood Classroom*. This book is widely used by early childhood center directors, curriculum specialists, teachers and students majoring in early childhood in colleges throughout the country. It emphasizes a developmental approach to thematic planning. Hundreds of activities for every occasion: art, social studies, finger plays, science, music, math, language arts, storybook and cooking are included in this excellent resource.

Using the Illustrations

The illustrations in this book can be used in many ways. For the early childhood classroom, the possibilities are endless. In addition to creating bulletin boards, you can use the outlines for:

labeling classroom areas and materials,
preparing charts,
creating large story board characters,
making puppets,
preparing flannel board pieces,
creating teacher-made games and
developing transparencies for storytelling.

50
Bulletin Boards

Alphabet Fish

Related Themes
Letters
Fish
Shapes
Communication

Alternate Titles
Fishing for Letters
Letter Fish

Materials
paper or fabric for background and border
colored tagboard
scissors
markers or crayons
contact paper or laminate
hole punch
map pins or cup hooks
basket, tray or box

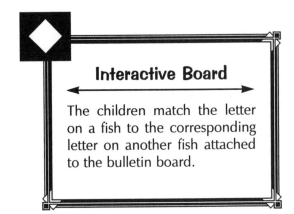

Interactive Board
The children match the letter on a fish to the corresponding letter on another fish attached to the bulletin board.

Preparation
1. Cover the background of the bulletin board with fabric, wrapping paper, construction paper or wallpaper.
2. Cut out, color and attach a border.
3. Trace, cut and attach letters to create the title.
4. Cut two sets of fish from colored tagboard.
5. Print a different letter on each set of fish.
6. Add details to each fish by drawing an eye and scales.
7. Cover the fish with clear contact paper or laminate.
8. Attach one set of fish to the board. Punch holes in the other set.
9. Put map pins or cup hooks on the set of fish attached to the bulletin board.
10. Put the other set of fish, the ones with holes punched in them, in a basket, tray or box adjacent to the bulletin board.

Variations
Vary the number of letters used depending on the developmental level of the children.
Use upper case letters on one set of fish and lower case letters on the matching fish.
Create a numeral match using the fish.

Alphabet Fish

Developmental Goals

To develop visual discrimination skills
To develop eye-hand coordination skills
To identify letters
To develop problem-solving skills

Big and Little

Related Themes
Sizes
Opposites
Big and little

Alternate Titles
My World
Sorting

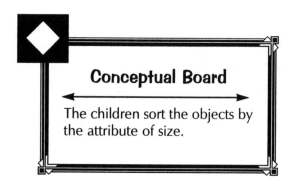

Conceptual Board

The children sort the objects by the attribute of size.

Materials
paper or fabric for background and border
construction paper
pencil, markers, crayons or craypas
opaque or overhead projector, optional
scissors
clear contact paper or laminate
masking tape
basket, tray or box

Preparation
1. Cover the background of the bulletin board with paper or fabric.
2. Cut out, color and attach a border, if desired.
3. Trace, cut and attach letters to create a title.
4. Sketch freehand or use an opaque or overhead projector to create two sets of objects, one large and one small, on construction paper. Suggestions for objects include an apple, ball, crayon, flower, shoe and car.
5. Cut out the objects.
6. Color and add details to the objects.
7. Cover all objects with clear contact paper or laminate.
8. Place masking tape and the objects in a basket, tray or box adjacent to the bulletin board.
9. The children put the big outlines on the side of the board labeled "big" and the little objects on the side of the board labeled "little." With young children, attach one or two examples to the board.

Variation
Design the board to use other classifications, such as fruits/vegetables, warm/cool, red/green.

Developmental Goals
To develop visual discrimination skills
To develop classification skills
To develop eye-hand coordination skills

Busy Beaver

Related Themes
Animals
Numbers
Pond animals

Alternate Title
Count the sticks.

Materials
paper or fabric for background and border
construction paper or tagboard
pencil, markers, crayons or craypas
opaque or overhead projector, optional
scissors
glue and sticks, optional
string or yarn
curtain rings
map pins or cup hooks

Interactive Board

The children match the string attached to the printed numeral to the box with the corresponding number of sticks.

Preparation
1. Cover the background of the board with fabric or paper.
2. Cut out, color and attach a border.
3. Cut letters for the title and numerals using the patterns included in this book.
4. Sketch freehand or use the opaque or overhead projector to enlarge and trace the beaver shape on construction paper or tagboard.
5. Color and add details to the beaver as desired.
6. Cut a set of squares from construction paper or tagboard.
7. Glue sets of sticks or draw them for each square. Use just a few squares with young children; add more squares as needed.
8. Attach beaver, squares and numerals to the board.
9. Cut a piece of string or yarn for each set of sticks. Tie a curtain ring to the bottom of each string. Attach each string to one of the squares with sticks.
10. Put a map pin or cup hook above each numeral.

Variations
Provide paper for the children to print the numeral representing the number of sticks.
Print individual cards with the name of each numeral.

Developmental Goals

To practice one-to-one correspondence skills
To develop visual discrimination skills
To develop eye-hand coordination skills
To develop problem-solving skills
To develop numeral recognition skills

Butterfly Sequencing

Related Themes
Nature
Insects
Sizes

Alternate Title
Beautiful Butterflies

Materials
paper or fabric for background and border
tagboard
pencil, markers, crayons or craypas
opaque or overhead projector, optional
scissors
hole punch
clear contact paper or laminate, optional
map pins or cup hooks
basket, tray or box

Preparation
1. Cover the board with paper or fabric.
2. Cut out, color and attach a border.
3. Trace, cut and attach letters on the board to create a title.
4. Sketch freehand or use the opaque or overhead projector to create twelve butterflies of varying sizes on tagboard as illustrated.
5. Cut out the butterflies and punch a hole near the top of each piece.
6. Color and decorate the butterflies.
7. Cover the butterflies with clear contact paper or laminate if desired.
8. Attach map pins or cup hooks to the board as illustrated.
9. Place the butterflies in a basket, tray or box adjacent to the board.

Variation
Choose other theme-related objects to draw in a variety of sizes and sequence the figures on the bulletin board.

Interactive Board

The children put the butterflies in sequence by size.

Developmental Goals

To develop left-to-right progression skills

To develop visual discrimination skills

To develop problem-solving skills

To develop sequencing skills

Color Sort

Related Themes
Art
Colors
Pictures
Communication

Alternate Titles
Colors
Sort by color.
Colors in Our World

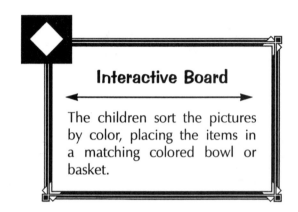

Interactive Board
The children sort the pictures by color, placing the items in a matching colored bowl or basket.

Materials
paper or fabric for background and border
construction paper or tagboard
pencil, markers, crayons or craypas
opaque or overhead projector, optional
scissors
magazines, catalogs, wrapping paper or greetings cards
clear contact paper or laminate
basket, tray or box

Preparation
1. Choose and attach a color of construction paper, material or crepe paper that will complement the bowls or baskets to the bulletin board.
2. Cut out, color and attach a border.
3. Trace, cut and attach letters for the bulletin board title.
4. Sketch freehand or use the opaque or overhead projector to trace a set of bowls or baskets on various colors of construction paper or tagboard.
5. Cut out the bowl shapes.
6. Using felt-tip markers, print the name of the color on each bowl or basket.
7. Trace and cut out objects that are the same colors as the colors of the bowls from construction paper or tagboard. Pictures of objects may also be cut from magazines, catalogs, wrapping paper or greeting cards.
8. Cover the bulletin board with clear contact paper or laminate.
9. Attach the bowls or baskets around the sides and bottom of the board, allowing the top edge to be open so that the children can insert the colored objects or pictures in the bowls or baskets.
10. Place the colored objects or pictures in a basket, tray or box adjacent to the bulletin board.

Variation
Vary the number of colors used according to the children's skills and abilities.

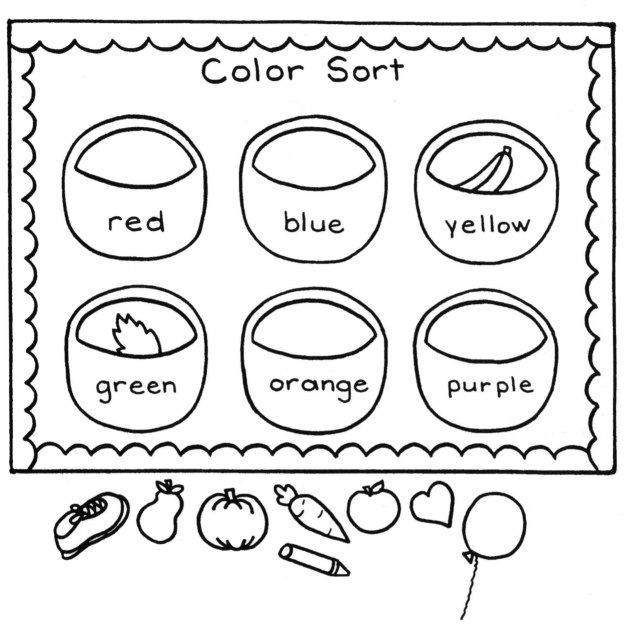

Developmental Goals

To practice classifying by color
To develop visual discrimination skills
To develop eye-hand coordination skills
To develop problem-solving skills
To develop small muscle coordination skills
To practice color recognition

The Computer Keyboard

Related Themes
Alphabet
Communication
Computers
Machines
Tools

Alternate Title
Computer Keys

Materials
paper or fabric for background and border
construction paper or tagboard
pencil, markers, crayons or craypas
opaque or overhead projector, optional
scissors
clear contact paper or laminate
masking tape
basket, tray or box

Interactive Board
The children match the letters and numerals to those on the computer keyboard.

Preparation
1. Cover the background of the bulletin board with paper or fabric.
2. Cut out, color and attach a border.
3. Trace, cut and attach letters to create the title.
4. Sketch freehand or use an opaque or overhead projector to create a computer keyboard on tagboard or construction paper.
5. Cut two sheets of small squares, as illustrated, to represent computer keys.
6. Using felt-tip markers, print two sets of letters. Cover the letters with clear contact paper or laminate.
7. Cut out the keys.
8. Glue one set of letters to the computer keys. If desired, laminate the computer outlines.
9. Place the other set of letters and masking tape in a basket, tray or box adjacent to the bulletin board.

Variations
Create the board using only the numeral or letter keys.
Create a set of lower case letters for matching the upper case letters on the keys.

The Computer Keyboard

Developmental Goals
To explore the computer keyboard
To practice letter and numeral recognition
To improve eye-hand coordination skills
To develop visual discrimination skills

Count the birthday candles.

Related Themes
Bakery
Celebrations
Foods
Numbers
Communications

Alternate Titles
Happy Birthday
A Birthday Cake

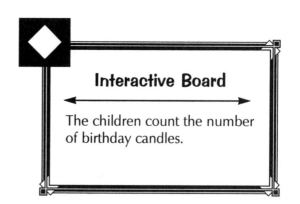

Interactive Board

The children count the number of birthday candles.

Materials
paper or fabric for the background and border
construction paper or tagboard
pencil, markers, crayons or craypas
opaque or overhead projector, optional
clear contact paper or laminate, optional
masking tape
basket, tray or box

Preparation
1. Choose and attach a background paper or fabric to the bulletin board that will complement the cakes.
2. Prepare or select a border and attach.
3. Trace, cut and attach letters for the title. If desired, apply clear contact paper or laminate.
4. Sketch freehand or use the opaque or overhead projector to trace two sets of birthday cakes on construction paper or tagboard.
5. Cut out the two sets of birthday cake outlines.
6. On one set add colorful details, such as frosting, decorations and a different number of candles.
7. On the other set of cakes, print the corresponding words that identify the number of candles.
8. Attach the set of birthday cakes that are labeled with the words identifying the number of candles to the bulletin board.
9. Place masking tape and the other set of decorated cakes in a basket, tray or box adjacent to the bulletin board.

Variations
The children can match one cake to another cake with the same number of candles on the bulletin board.
Vary the number of cakes to make the activity developmentally appropriate for younger or older children.
Use different colors of frosting and encourage the children to match the color and design of the frosting.

Count the birthday candles.

Developmental Goals

To associate a numeral with a set of objects
To practice eye-hand coordination skills
To identify the printed words for the numerals 1 to 6
To develop small muscle coordination skills
To practice problem-solving skills
To develop visual discrimination skills

Count the bones.

Related Themes
Dogs
Pets
Animals
Nursery rhymes

Alternate Titles
Feed the dog.
Give the dog a bone.

Materials
paper or fabric for background and border
construction paper or tagboard
pencil, markers, crayons or craypas
opaque or overhead projector, optional
clear contact paper or laminate, optional
basket, tray or box

Interactive Board
The children place the correct number of dog bones in each bowl.

Preparation
1. Cover the bulletin board with colored paper that will complement the bowls.
2. Prepare or select a border and attach it to the board.
3. Trace, cut and attach bulletin board letters for the title.
4. Sketch freehand or use the opaque or overhead projector to trace the dog, bowls and bones onto colored construction paper or tagboard.
5. Cut out the dog, bowls and bones.
6. Color and add details to the dog.
7. On each bowl, print a numeral and the corresponding word.
8. If desired, apply clear contact paper or laminate.
9. Cut a wide slit on the top of each bowl, allowing a space for the children to insert the bones.
10. Attach the bowls and dog as illustrated.
11. Place the bones in a basket, tray or box adjacent to the bulletin board.

Variations
Depending on the children's developmental levels, the numerals used can be increased or
    decreased.
Prepare colored dog tags and bowls for the children to match.

Developmental Goals

To practice numeral recognition skills
To practice counting skills
To practice decision-making skills
To improve eye-hand coordination skills
To develop visual discrimination skills

Count the teddy bears.

Related Themes
Bears
Toys
Zoo animals

Alternate Titles
Teddy Bear Count
Bears
Matching

Materials
paper or fabric for background and border
construction paper or tagboard
pencil, markers, crayons or craypas
opaque or overhead projector, optional
scissors
clear contact paper or laminate, optional
masking tape
grease pencils
piece of felt
basket, tray or box

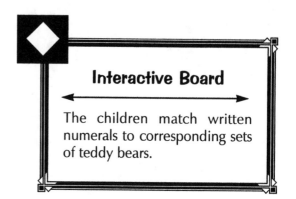

Interactive Board
The children match written numerals to corresponding sets of teddy bears.

Preparation
1. Cover the bulletin board with a paper or fabric.
2. Attach a border, if desired.
3. Trace, cut and attach letters on the board to create a title.
4. Sketch freehand or use the opaque or overhead projector to trace 21 teddy bears on colored construction paper or tagboard.
5. Cut out the teddy bears.
6. Color and add details, such as eyes, nose, paws to the bears.
7. If desired, cover the bears with clear contact paper or laminate.
8. Cut sets of squares from colored construction paper or tagboard.
9. On one set of squares, print the numerals as illustrated.
10. Using 1" strips of colored paper, divide the bulletin board into six sections as illustrated.
11. Attach a blank square in the upper left corner of each of the six sections as illustrated.
12. If developmentally appropriate, with a felt-tip marker, using broken lines, print the numeral to the right of each blank square as illustrated.
13. Place masking tape, grease pencils, a piece of felt to wipe away marks and the squares containing the numerals in a basket, tray or box adjacent to the bulletin board.

Variation

Increase or decrease the number of bears.

Developmental Goals

To practice decoding symbols
To match numerals to corresponding sets of objects
To develop visual discrimination skills
To develop problem-solving skills

Decorate a pumpkin.

Related Themes
Halloween
Foods
Parties
Holidays
Communications

Alternate Titles
Halloween Faces
Parties

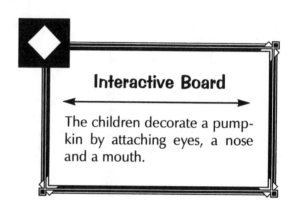

Interactive Board

The children decorate a pumpkin by attaching eyes, a nose and a mouth.

Materials
felt or construction paper for background and border
felt, tagboard or construction paper
pencil, markers, crayons or craypas
opaque or overhead projector, optional
scissors
heavy paper
clear contact paper or laminate if shapes are from paper
velcro
resealable plastic bag

Preparation
1. Cover the bulletin board with felt or construction paper.
2. Add a complementary border.
3. Trace, cut and attach letters to create the title.
4. Sketch freehand or use the opaque or overhead projector to create six different pumpkin shapes on felt, tagboard or construction paper.
5. Cut out the pumpkin shapes.
6. Cut different shapes of eye, nose and mouth pieces from felt, tagboard or construction paper.
7. Cut three 4"x6" rectangles from heavy paper. Label one rectangle "eyes," one rectangle "nose" and one rectangle "mouth."
8. Color and add any desired details to pumpkins.
9. Cover with clear contact paper or laminate the facial features of the pumpkin and rectangles if constructed from tagboard or paper.
10. Attach the pumpkins and rectangle pockets as illustrated.
11. Put velcro on the fronts of the pumpkins and on the backs of the eye, nose and mouth pieces.
12. Place the eye, nose and mouth pieces in their respective pockets.

Variation
Create a decorative bulletin board by using the caption of Halloween and attaching a large
 pumpkin face.

Developmental Goals
To develop eye-hand coordination skills
To practice visual discrimination skills
To develop problem-solving skills
To develop small muscle coordination skills

Decorate the clown faces.

Related Themes
Clowns
Costumes
Circus

Alternate Title
Make a face.

Materials
fabric or paper for the background and border
heavy weight paper or tagboard
pencil, markers, crayons or craypas
opaque or overhead projector, optional
scissors
velcro

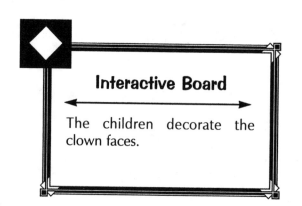

Interactive Board

The children decorate the clown faces.

Preparation
1. Cover the background of the board with fabric, wrapping paper, construction paper or wallpaper.
2. Prepare or select a border and attach it to the board.
3. Trace, cut and attach letters to create a title.
4. Sketch freehand or use an opaque or overhead projector to create three oval face shapes and a clown hat on tagboard or heavy weight paper.
5. Use colored felt-tip markers to add hair, eyes, nose, mouth and teeth. Also add decorations to the hat.
6. Cut five 5"x6" cards. Label each with a different body part or accessory: eyes, noses, mouths, hair and hats. Attach to the board, keeping the top open for inserting pieces.
7. Cut two different eye shapes from tagboard. Using a felt-tip marker, color one brown and the other blue. Continue preparing noses, hair, hats and mouth pieces. Color the hair, hats, noses and mouth pieces different colors.
8. Attach 1/4" velcro strips to the clown faces, facial features and hats.
9. Place the hats and facial features in the five holders.

Variations
Add a variety of other decorations for the clown including different hats, glasses and bow ties.
Add shadows of the clown faces to create another interactive bulletin board.

Decorate the clown faces.

| eyes | noses | mouths | hair | hats |

Developmental Goals

To practice letter recognition skills
To develop visual discrimination skills
To practice decoding words
To develop hand-eye coordination

Dice Match

Related Themes
Games
Numbers
Shapes

Alternate Titles
Count the dots.
Match the dice.

Materials
construction paper or fabric for background
    and border
construction paper or tagboard
pencil, markers, crayons or craypas
opaque or overhead projector, optional
scissors
string or yarn
curtain rings
map pins or cup hooks

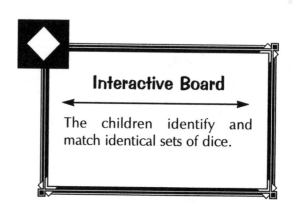

Interactive Board

The children identify and match identical sets of dice.

Preparation
1. Cover the bulletin board background with colored construction paper or fabric. Add a border if desired.
2. Trace and cut letters from fabric or paper and attach to the bulletin board to create a title.
3. Sketch freehand or use the opaque or overhead projector to create two sets of dice from tagboard or construction paper.
4. Cut out the dice shapes.
5. Using a felt-tip marker, code the dice by applying dots. Prepare two identical sets.
6. Place one set of dice vertically along the left side of the bulletin board as illustrated.
7. Scatter the second set of dice toward the right side of the board as illustrated.
8. Attach a piece of string or yarn with a curtain ring to each of the dice on the left side of the bulletin board.
9. Attach a map pin or cup hook to each of the randomly placed dice on the right side.

Variations
Use a different color for each set of dice, making the board a color matching activity.
Line up the dice in numerical order, creating a counting board.

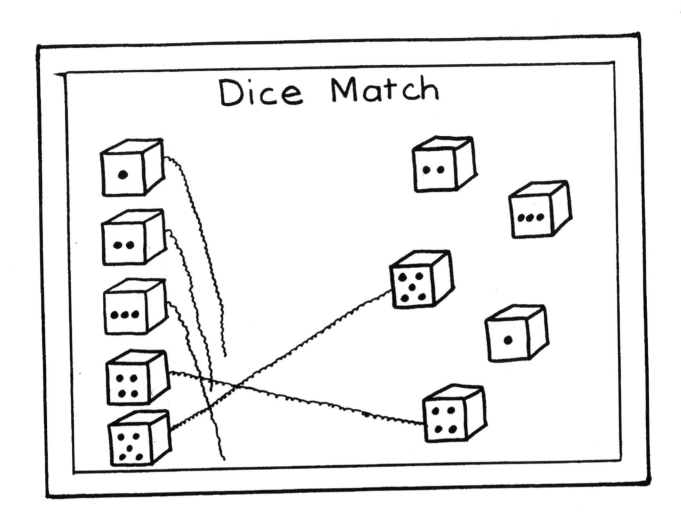

Developmental Goals

To practice one-to-one correspondence skills
To develop eye-hand coordination skills
To develop problem-solving skills
To develop visual discrimination skills

Fill the cookie jars.

Related Themes
Cookies
Foods
Containers
Numbers

Alternate Title
Cookie Count

Materials
paper or fabric for background and border
construction paper or tagboard
pencil, markers, crayons or craypas
opaque or overhead projector, optional
scissors
velcro

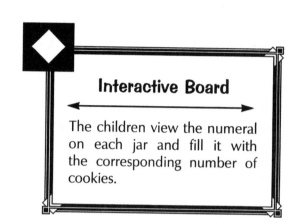

Interactive Board

The children view the numeral on each jar and fill it with the corresponding number of cookies.

Preparation
1. Cover the background of the bulletin board with paper or fabric.
2. Cut and attach a border.
3. Trace, cut and attach letters to create a title.
4. Sketch freehand or use the overhead or opaque projector to trace eleven cookie jars and at least fifteen cookies.
5. Use a felt-tip marker to print a numeral and its corresponding symbol on each cookie jar as illustrated.
6. Attach 1/4" strip of velcro to the front of cookie jars and backs of the cookies.
7. Attach the cookie jars to the bulletin board, velcro side out.
8. Put the cookies in a basket, tray or box adjacent to the bulletin board.

Variation
Depending on the children's developmental levels, add or reduce the number of cookie jars.

Developmental Goals

To practice numeral recognition skills
To associate the printed word with a numeral
To develop eye-hand coordination skills
To develop visual discrimination skills
To practice decoding written symbols
To develop small muscle coordination skills

Find my acorns.

Related Themes
Woodland animals
Seeds and nuts

Alternate Titles
Squirrels
Squirrels and Acorns

Materials
construction paper or fabric for background
construction paper or tagboard
pencil, markers, crayons or craypas
opaque or overhead projector, optional
scissors
map pins or cup hooks
string, yarn or ribbon
curtain rings

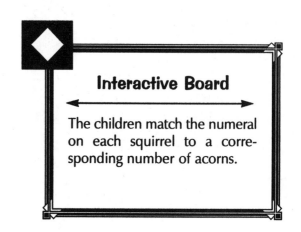

Interactive Board
The children match the numeral on each squirrel to a corresponding number of acorns.

Preparation
1. Cover the bulletin board with colored construction paper or fabric.
2. Trace, cut and add details to acorns to create a border. Attach as illustrated.
3. Trace, cut and attach letters to create a title.
4. Sketch freehand or use the opaque or overhead projector to trace squirrels on construction paper or tagboard. Cut out the squirrels.
5. Color and add details, such as facial features and a numeral on each squirrel.
6. Cut out a 7"x7" square for each squirrel. Draw the number of acorns on each square to correspond to the numeral on each squirrel.
7. Attach the squirrels and cardboard squares to the bulletin board as illustrated. At the top of each cardboard square, attach a map pin or cup hook.
8. Cut a piece of string, ribbon or yarn for each squirrel and attach a curtain ring to the end. Attach one string to each squirrel.

Variation
Vary the number of acorn sets according to the children's skills and abilities.

Find my acorns.

Developmental Goals

To practice numeral recognition
To improve counting skills
To improve eye-hand coordination skills
To identify printed symbols

Firefighter Numbers

Related Themes
Community Helpers
Hats
Firefighters
Numbers
Safety
Occupations
Sets
Communication

Alternate Title
Match the numbers on the helmets.

Materials
fabric or paper for background and border
construction paper or tagboard
pencil, markers, crayons or craypas
scissors
opaque or overhead projector, optional
clear contact paper or laminate
masking tape
basket, tray or box

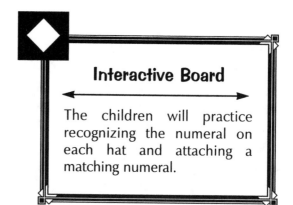

Interactive Board

The children will practice recognizing the numeral on each hat and attaching a matching numeral.

Preparation
1. Attach fabric or construction paper to cover the background of the bulletin board. Add a border, if desired.
2. Trace, cut and attach letters to create the title.
3. Sketch freehand or use an opaque or overhead projector to trace twelve firefighter hats on construction paper or tagboard.
4. Draw and cut two sets of twelve badges for the hats.
5. Using felt-tip markers, print numerals on one set of badges. On the other set of badges, draw a corresponding number of dots to match the numerals as illustrated. Attach the badges with dots to the hats.
6. Cover the hats with clear contact paper or laminate.
7. Put masking tape and the other set of badges in a basket, tray or box adjacent to the bulletin board.

Variation
If developmentally appropriate, ask the children to print the numerals on the hats.

Firefighter Numbers

Developmental Goals
To practice numeral recognition skills
To practice one-to-one correspondence skills
To develop visual discrimination skills
To develop problem-solving skills
To develop eye-hand coordination skills
To develop small muscle coordination skills

Frog Alphabet Match

Related Themes
Pond life
Letters
The alphabet
My world

Alternate Titles
Find a frog.
Can you match the frogs to the lily pads?

Interactive Board

The children match the letter on the frog to the corresponding letter on the lily pad attached to the bulletin board.

Materials
construction paper or fabric for background and border
construction paper or tagboard
pencil, markers, crayons or craypas
opaque or overhead projector, optional
scissors
clear contact paper or laminate, optional
hole punch
map pins or cup hooks
basket, tray or box

Preparation
1. Using construction paper or fabric cover the background of the bulletin board. Add a border, if desired.
2. Trace, cut and attach letters to create the title.
3. Sketch freehand or use the opaque or overhead projector to trace twelve frogs and twelve lily pads on tagboard or construction paper.
4. Color and add details, such as eyes, mouth and feet to the frogs.
5. Print a different letter on each frog. Print a corresponding letter on each of the lily pads.
6. Apply clear contact paper or laminate if desired.
7. Attach the lily pads to the board as illustrated.
8. Punch a hole in each frog.
9. Put a map pin or cup hook at the top of each lily pad.
10. Place the frogs in a basket, tray or box adjacent to the bulletin board.

Variations
Replace numerals with letters.
Use lower case letters.

Frog Alphabet Match

Developmental Goals
To practice eye-hand coordination skills
To practice letter recognition skills
To practice visual discrimination skills
To develop problem-solving skills
To develop small muscle coordination skills

Funny Clown Faces

Related Themes
Halloween
Entertainment
Faces
Body parts
Acting
Costumes

Alternate Titles
Create a clown face.
Make a funny clown.

Materials
paper or fabric for border and background
construction paper or tagboard
pencil, markers, crayons or craypas
opaque or overhead projector, optional
scissors
clear contact paper or laminate, optional
map pins or cup hooks
basket, tray or box

Interactive Board

The children identify and match identical sets of clown faces.

Preparation
1. Cover the bulletin board with construction paper or fabric.
2. Add a complementary border.
3. Trace, cut and attach letters to create the title.
4. Sketch freehand or use the opaque or overhead projector to create two sets of five clown faces and collars on colored construction paper or tagboard. Use red, blue, yellow, orange and purple. Make two clowns of each color.
5. Cut out the clown faces and collars.
6. Add hair by making circular scribbles with colored felt-tip markers. Decorate each pair the same.
7. Cover the faces with clear contact paper or laminate if desired.
8. Attach one set of the clown faces as illustrated. Write the color word under each clown as illustrated.
9. Put a map pin or cup hook at the top of each clown face on the bulletin board.
10. Punch a hole in the other set of clown faces.
11. Put the set of clown faces with the holes in a basket, tray or box adjacent to the bulletin board.

Funny Clown Faces

red blue yellow orange purple

Variations
Use symbols on the clown hats.
Print the names of colors on the clown hats.

Developmental Goals
To practice eye-hand coordination skills
To develop visual discrimination skills
To practice letter recognition skills

Gift Boxes

Related Themes
Celebrations
Gifts
Symbols
Holidays
Colors
Design

Alternate Titles
Gifts
Match the gift.

Materials
paper or fabric for background and border
construction paper or tagboard
pencil, markers, crayons or craypas
opaque or overhead projector, optional
scissors
clear contact paper or laminate
map pins or cup hooks
string
curtain rings

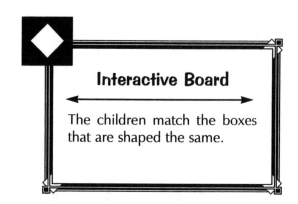

Interactive Board
The children match the boxes that are shaped the same.

Preparation
1. Cover the bulletin board with construction paper or fabric in a color that will complement the gift packages.
2. Add an attractive border.
3. Trace, cut and attach letters to create the title.
4. Sketch freehand or use the opaque or overhead projector to create two identical sets of gift boxes on tagboard or colored construction paper.
5. Cut out the gift boxes.
6. Color and add details, such as ribbons and bows to the boxes. Make each pair the same.
7. Cover the gift boxes with clear contact paper or laminate.
8. Attach one set of gift boxes vertically on the left side of the bulletin board. To each of these boxes, attach a string to which a curtain ring has been tied as illustrated.
9. Randomly attach the other set of gift boxes vertically on the right side of the bulletin board.
10. Place a map pin or cup hook next to each box.

Variation
Provide bows and encourage the children to place them on the boxes.

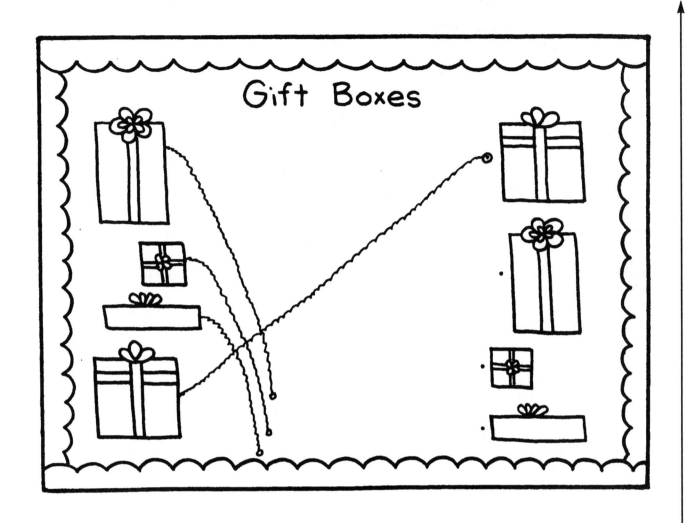

Gift Boxes

Developmental Goals
To develop eye-hand coordination skills
To develop one-to-one correspondence skills
To develop visual discrimination skills
To develop color identification skills
To develop problem-solving skills

Gingerbread People

Related Themes
The bakery
Foods
Hobbies
Stories
Fairy tales
Feelings

Alternate Title
Match the gingerbread people.

Materials
paper or fabric for background and border
construction paper or tagboard
pencil, markers, crayons or craypas
opaque or overhead projector, optional
scissors
clear contact paper or laminate
string, yarn or ribbon
curtain rings
map pins or cup hooks

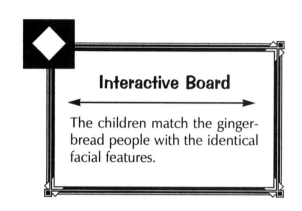

Interactive Board

The children match the gingerbread people with the identical facial features.

Preparation
1. Cover the background of the bulletin board with construction paper or fabric in a color that will complement the gingerbread people.
2. Add an attractive border.
3. Trace, cut and attach letters to create a title.
4. Sketch freehand or use the opaque or overhead projector to create five identical sets of gingerbread people on tagboard or colored construction paper.
5. Cut out the sets of gingerbread people.
6. Color and add details, such as eyes, nose, mouth, buttons and trim to each set of gingerbread people. Make each set identical but different from the other sets.
7. Cover the gingerbread people with clear contact paper or laminate.
8. Separate the five sets of gingerbread people. Attach one set to the left side of the bulletin board. Randomly attach the other set, as illustrated, to the right side of the board.
9. Cut a piece of string, ribbon or yarn for each set of gingerbread people. Attach a curtain ring to the end of each piece of string.
10. Secure one string to each of the gingerbread people on the left side of the bulletin board.
11. Put a map pin or cup hook next to each gingerbread person on the right side of the bulletin board.

Gingerbread People

Variation
Cut the gingerbread people from different colored materials.

Developmental Goals
To develop visual discrimination skills
To develop eye-hand coordination skills
To develop problem-solving skills
To practice one-to-one correspondence

The Growth of a Flower

Related Themes
Flowers
Gardens
Seeds
Plant growth

Alternate Title
Flower Growth

Materials
background and border paper or fabric
tagboard
pencil, markers, crayons or craypas
scissors
clear contact paper or laminate, optional

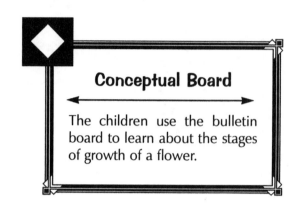

Conceptual Board
The children use the bulletin board to learn about the stages of growth of a flower.

Preparation
1. Cover the bulletin board with fabric or paper that complements the environment.
2. Cut a strip border 3" wide.
3. Using colored felt-tip markers or flower stickers, decorate the border. Attach the border.
4. Trace, cut and attach letters to create a title.
5. Cut four 12"x14" rectangles from tagboard.
6. On each rectangle represent a different stage of plant growth, such as seed sprouting, development of the root system, development of the stem and development of the flower.
7. If desired, cover the rectangles with clear contact paper or laminate.
8. Sequentially attach the four stages of growth to the bulletin board.

Variations
Illustrate other types of plant growth, such as vegetables, fruits and trees.
Create an interactive bulletin board by preparing two sets of identical rectangles with the different stages of plant growth. Punch a hole at the top of one set and add map pins or cup hooks to the bulletin board. Ask the children to match the rectangles to each stage of plant growth.

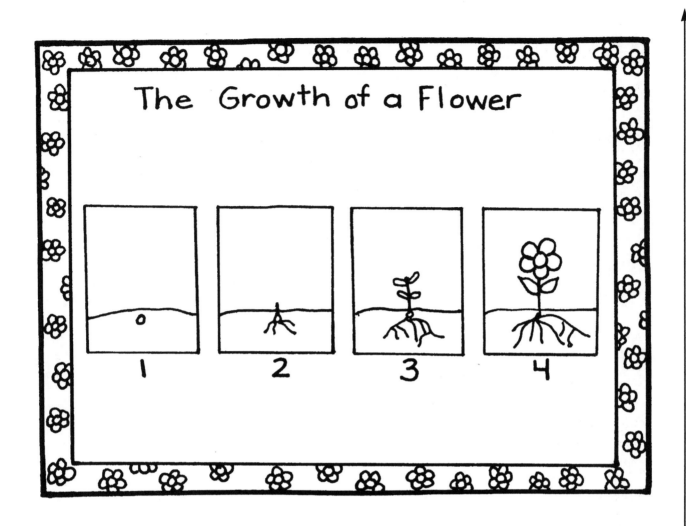

The Growth of a Flower

1   2   3   4

Developmental Goals

To learn the stages of plant growth
To learn the parts of a plant
To develop visual discrimination skills
To develop an appreciation of nature

Hammers and Nails

Related Themes
Carpenter
Construction
Community helpers
Tools
Numbers

Alternate Titles
Count the nails.
Hammer Match

Materials
paper or fabric for background and border
construction paper or tagboard
scissors
pencil, markers, crayons or craypas
opaque or overhead projector, optional
black construction paper, optional
glue
clear contact paper or laminate
velcro
box or resealable plastic bag

Interactive Board

The children count the number of nails on each rectangle and hang the hammer with the corresponding numeral next to the rectangle.

Preparation
1. Cover the bulletin board background with construction paper or fabric. Add a border, if desired.
2. Trace, cut and attach letters to create the title.
3. Cut ten 8"x10" rectangles from colored construction paper or tagboard.
4. Sketch freehand or use the opaque or overhead projector to trace a hammer and nail(s) on each rectangle as illustrated.
5. Sketch and cut ten additional hammers. Print the numerals across the bottom of each rectangle as illustrated.
6. Using a felt-tip marker, shade in the hammer and nails. Another option is to cut the hammer and nail shapes from black construction paper and glue the shapes onto the rectangles.
7. Print a numeral on each handle of the second set of hammers.
8. Draw the nails vertically on the left side of the rectangle.
9. Cover the individual hammers and rectangles with clear contact paper or laminate.
10. Attach the rectangles to the board as illustrated.
11. Attach velcro to the backs of individual hammers and to the front of the hammers on the bulletin board. Place the individual hammers in a tray, box or resealable plastic bag and place adjacent to the bulletin board.

Variations

Vary the number of hammers and nails used according to the developmental level of the children.
Create the nail board using roofing nails.

Developmental Goals

To develop numeral recognition skills
To develop one-to-one correspondence skills
To develop eye-hand coordination skills
To develop problem-solving skills
To develop visual discrimination skills

The Ice Cream Shop

Related Themes
Food
Nutrition
Summer fun
Celebrations

Alternate Titles
Ice Cream
Sundae Shop

Materials
paper or fabric for background and border
construction paper or tagboard
pencil, markers, crayons or craypas
opaque or overhead projector, optional
scissors
clear contact paper or laminate
map pins or cup hooks
hole punch
basket, tray or box

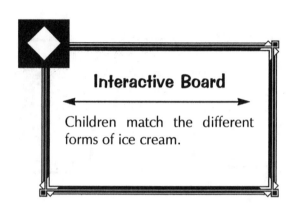

Interactive Board

Children match the different forms of ice cream.

Preparation
1. Cover the bulletin board with colored construction paper or in fabric that will complement the ice cream outlines. Add a border, if desired.
2. Trace, cut and attach letters to create the title.
3. Sketch freehand or use the opaque or overhead projector to draw two sets of the ice cream novelties and the awning onto tagboard or construction paper.
4. Cut out ice cream novelties.
5. Color and decorate the novelties, making each pair identical, and add details to the awning.
6. Cover the ice cream novelties with clear contact paper or laminate if desired.
7. Attach one set of ice cream novelties and the awning to the bulletin board.
8. Put a map pin or cup hook at the top of each ice cream novelty.
9. Punch a hole in the other set of matching novelties.
10. Put the set of novelties with the hole in a basket, tray or box adjacent to the bulletin board.

Variations
Add utensils used at an ice cream shop.
Provide printed identification labels for the children to hang under each ice cream novelty item.

Developmental Goals

To identify the ways ice cream can be served
To recognize different types of ice cream toppings
To develop letter recognition skills
To develop visual discrimination skills

Look at our marble paintings.

Related Themes
Creativity
Colors
Art
Painting

Alternate Titles
Painting
Painting with Marbles
Amazing Artists

Child-Created Board

Children add their artwork to the bulletin board.

Materials
corrugated paper, construction paper, cork or tagboard
scissors
paint in shallow trays
containers
paper to fit container
marbles

Preparation
1. Cover the background of the bulletin board with colored corrugated paper, construction paper, cork or tagboard.
2. Create and cut a scalloped border to add interest.
3. Trace, cut and attach letters to create a title.
4. Provide the children with paint in shallow trays, paper that is cut to fit the container and marbles. Caution: With young children who still put things in their mouths, provide close supervision when the children are working with marbles.
5. After the children finish their marble paintings, hang the paintings up to dry.
6. When the paintings are dry, attach them to the bulletin board.

Variations
Try painting with different objects, such as blocks, sponges, cookie cutters, leaves and bones.
Use seasonal or holiday paintings.
Change the title to "Collage" and provide materials for the children to create their own collage artwork.

Developmental Goals

To develop an appreciation of art process
To develop eye-hand coordination
To experiment with different ways of painting
To develop creativity

Magic Rabbits

Related Themes
Letters
Animals
Easter
Pets
Hats
Rabbits

Alternate Titles
Alphabet Rabbits
Rabbit Friends

Materials
paper or fabric for background
construction paper or tagboard
pencil, markers, crayons or craypas
opaque or overhead projector, optional
scissors
clear contact paper or laminate
stapler
basket, tray or box

Interactive Board
The children pull one rabbit at a time from the hat on the board and identify the letter on its chest.

Preparation
1. Cover the bulletin board with construction paper or fabric.
2. Trace, cut and attach letters to create the title.
3. Sketch freehand or use the opaque or overhead projector to trace one hat, 52 rabbits and enough carrots to make the border on colored construction paper or tagboard.
4. Cut out the hat, rabbits and carrots.
5. Color and add facial features to the rabbits including eyes, nose, mouth and whiskers. Outline the rabbits ears. Then print a different letter on each rabbit.
6. Cover the rabbits with clear contact paper or laminate.
7. Staple the carrots around the four outside edges of the bulletin board to create a border as illustrated.
8. Cut a circle inside the hat's brim.
9. Attach the hat to the board, carefully stapling the outside perimeter, leaving space for the rabbits.
10. To add interest, glue a carrot on the lower right side of the hat as illustrated.
11. Place the rabbits in a basket, tray or box adjacent to the bulletin board.

Variations
Vary the number of letters used according to the developmental level of the children.
On one set of rabbits print upper case letters and on the other set of rabbits print lower case letters. Encourage the children to match the upper and lower case letters.

Magic Rabbits

Developmental Goals

To recognize letters
To develop small muscle control
To improve eye-hand coordination skills
To develop problem-solving skills
To develop visual discrimination skills

Make a puppet.

Related Themes
Art
Puppets
Communication
Creativity
Fairy tales
Stories
Storytelling

Alternate Titles
Puppet Factory
Puppet Fun

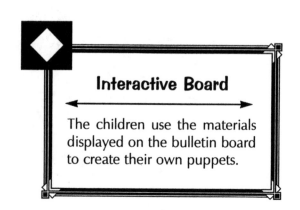

Interactive Board
The children use the materials displayed on the bulletin board to create their own puppets.

Materials
paper or fabric for background and border
paper bags, fabric scraps, tongue depressors and yarn
construction paper
scissors
markers
staplers
tray or basket
glue

Preparation
1. Cover the bulletin board with construction paper or fabric.
2. Cut and add a scalloped border to add interest.
3. Trace, cut and attach letters to create the title.
4. Collect paper bags, paper, fabric scraps, tongue depressors and yarn.
5. Cut two 8"x10" rectangles from colored construction paper to hold the paper bags and paper. Using a felt-tip marker, print "paper" on one rectangle and "paper bags" on the other.
6. Cut three 14"x10" rectangles from colored construction paper. Fold each rectangle to measure 8"x10", forming a pocket. Staple the outside edge of each rectangle to form a pocket. On the first rectangle print "fabric," on the second print "tongue depressors" and on the third print "yarn."
7. Attach the five containers to the board as illustrated. Fill each container.
8. Create a paper bag puppet. Add yarn for hair. Using felt-tip markers, add eyes and a nose. Cut lips from red construction paper and glue onto the puppet. Attach the paper bag puppet to the bulletin board as an example.
9. Create a cat puppet using a tongue depressor. Draw and cut the head from construction paper. Using a felt-tip marker, add eyes, nose and a mouth. Cut pieces of yarn and glue onto the face for whiskers. Attach the puppet to the bulletin board as an example.
10. In a tray or basket adjacent to the bulletin board place scissors, glue, staplers and felt-tip markers.

Variations

Add glove fingers to create finger puppets.
Place a puppet theater next to the board to encourage use of the newly created puppets.

Developmental Goals

To communicate through creative dramatics
To develop creativity
To experiment with a variety of art materials
To develop problem-solving skills
To develop language skills

Make a word.

Related Themes
Communications
Letters
Word families
Words
Sounds
Writing
Writing tools

Alternate Titles
Words
Word Families

Materials
paper or fabric for background and border
construction paper or tagboard
pencil, markers, crayons or craypas
opaque or overhead projector, optional
scissors
hole punch
map pins or cup hooks
basket, tray or resealable plastic bag

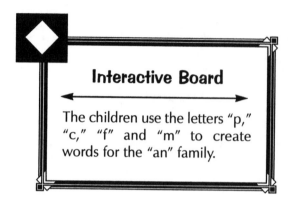

Interactive Board
The children use the letters "p," "c," "f" and "m" to create words for the "an" family.

Preparation
1. Cover the bulletin board with construction paper or fabric.
2. Create and attach a scalloped border to the bulletin board.
3. Using the letter patterns in this book, trace and cut out letters for the title and for the name of each object. Attach the letters to create a title.
4. Sketch freehand or use an opaque or overhead projector to trace a pan, fan, man and can onto construction paper or tagboard.
5. Cut out the pan, fan, man and can.
6. Color and add details to the pan, fan, man and can.
7. Cut out eight squares that are larger than letters.
8. Glue the letters "m," "p," "c" and "f" on four of the squares, one letter to a square. Punch a hole in the top of each of these four squares. Leave four squares blank.
9. Attach the four objects. In front of each, attach a blank square followed by letters "a" and "n" as illustrated. Put a map pin or cup hook at the top of each blank square.
10. Place the letters "m," "p," "c" and "f" in a basket, tray or resealable plastic bag attached to the bulletin board.

Variations
Use only if developmentally appropriate with the children in you class.
Use the same format for the "at," "and" and "it" families.
Add more beginning sounds with corresponding pictures.

Developmental Goals
To become familiar with word families
To observe a print/rich environment
To review the sounds of letters
To practice forming letters
To practice left-to-right progression skills
To practice decoding the written word

Match the bees to their hives.

Related Themes
Bees
Nature
Food sources

Alternate Title
Place the bees in their hives.

Materials
paper or fabric for background and border
construction paper or tagboard
pencil, markers, crayons or craypas
opaque or overhead projector, optional
scissors
clear contact paper or laminate
hole punch
map pin or cup hook
basket, tray or box

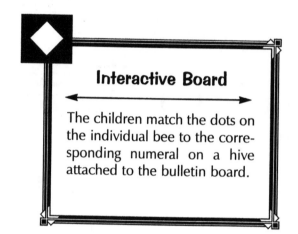

Interactive Board

The children match the dots on the individual bee to the corresponding numeral on a hive attached to the bulletin board.

Preparation
1. Cover the bulletin board with colored construction paper or fabric that will complement the bees and hives. Add a border, if desired.
2. Trace, cut and attach letters to create a title.
3. Sketch freehand or use the opaque or overhead projector to trace ten bees and ten beehives onto colored construction paper or tagboard.
4. Cut out the individual bees and beehives.
5. Color and add details to the hives and bees as illustrated. Beginning with numeral one and continuing to ten, print a different numeral on each hive. Then repeat making round black circles to represent each of the numerals on the bees.
6. Cover the bees and hives with clear contact paper or laminate.
7. Randomly attach the hives to the bulletin board as illustrated.
8. Punch a hole in the top of each bee.
9. Put a cup hook or map pin at the top of each hive.
10. Place the bees in a basket, tray or box adjacent to the board.

Variations
Use upper and/or lower case letters.
Draw a shape on each hive and a similar shape on each bee.

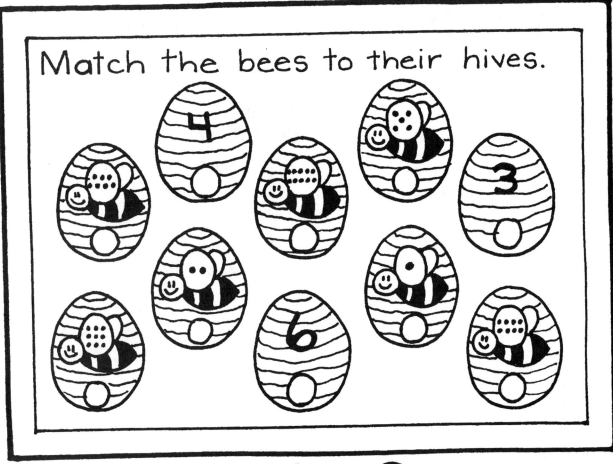

Match the bees to their hives.

Developmental Goals

To associate bees with hives
To develop eye-hand coordination skills
To develop visual discrimination skills
To develop one-to-one correspondence skills
To develop problem-solving skills

Match the rhyming words.

Related Themes
Words
Rhymes
Matching
Communication
Books
Listening

Alternate Titles
Rhyming Words
Words That Rhyme

Materials
paper or fabric for background and border
construction paper or tagboard
pencil, markers, crayons or craypas
opaque or overhead projector, optional
scissors
string
curtain rings
map pins or cup hooks

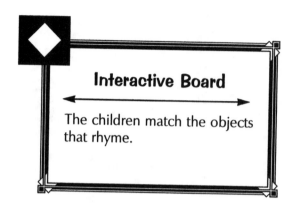

Interactive Board
The children match the objects that rhyme.

Preparation
1. Cover the bulletin board with construction paper or fabric.
2. Create, cut and attach a border.
3. Trace, cut and attach letters to create the title.
4. Sketch freehand or use the opaque or overhead projector to trace a cake, bee, can, mouse, house, frog, tree, snake, fan and log onto colored construction paper or tagboard.
5. Cut out the figures.
6. Color and add details to the figures as illustrated.
7. Attach vertically on the left side of the board the cake, bee, can, log and mouse. On the right side of the board attach the house, frog, tree, snake and fan.
8. Cut five pieces of string long enough to reach from the objects attached on the left side of the board to the right side of the board. To one end of each of the pieces of string attach a curtain ring.
9. Attach one piece of string to each outline on the left side of the board.
10. Put a map pin or cup hook next to each object on the right, providing the children a hook on which to place the curtain ring.

Variation
If developmentally appropriate, print the name of the object and encourage the children to hang the string on the name adjacent to the object.

Developmental Goals

To practice recognizing rhyming words
To develop visual discrimination skills
To practice eye-hand coordination skills
To practice problem-solving skills

The Muffin Man

Related Themes
Bakery
Food
Nursery rhymes
Baked goods
Breakfast foods
Breads

Alternate Titles
Muffins
Our Class

Materials
paper or fabric for background
construction paper or tagboard
pencil, markers, crayons or craypas
opaque or overhead projector, optional
scissors
clear contact paper or laminate
hole punch
map pins or cup hooks
basket, tray or box

Interactive Board
The children place their muffin name tag on the bulletin board upon arriving at the center or school each day.

Preparation
1. Cover the bulletin board with construction paper or fabric. Add a border, if desired.
2. Trace, cut and attach letters to create the title.
3. Sketch freehand or use the opaque or overhead projector to trace the baker and one muffin for each child in the class on tagboard or construction paper.
4. Cut out the outlines of the baker and muffins.
5. Color and add details to the muffins. Then print each child's name on a muffin.
6. Cover the baker and the muffins with clear contact paper or laminate.
7. Punch a hole in each muffin.
8. Center and attach the baker to the bulletin board as illustrated.
9. Put map pins or cup hooks on the bulletin board so the children can hang their muffins.
10. Place the muffins in a basket, tray or box adjacent to the bulletin board.

Variations
Ask the children to create their own muffins.
Create a border using commercially purchased colored paper muffin cups.

Developmental Goals

To practice following directions
To distinguish their name from others
To learn the names of other children
To develop an appreciation of the printed word
To develop problem-solving skills
To develop letter recognition skills
To develop positive self-esteem

My School Friends

Related Themes
Photography
Friends
School

Alternate Titles
Friends
Our Class
We're special.

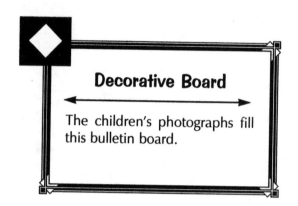

Decorative Board

The children's photographs fill this bulletin board.

Materials
paper or fabric for background and border
construction paper or tagboard
pencil, markers, crayons or craypas
opaque or overhead projector, optional
scissors
photographs of the children
clear contact paper or laminate, optional

Preparation
1. Cover the background of the bulletin board with construction paper or fabric. Add a border, if desired.
2. Trace, cut and attach letters to create the title.
3. Sketch freehand or use the opaque or overhead projector to create the tree, bucket and individual apples on tagboard or construction paper. Make one apple for each child in the class.
4. Cut out the tree, bucket and apples.
5. Attach the tree and bucket to the bulletin board.
6. Glue a picture of each child to an individual apple. If desired, cover with clear contact paper or laminate.
7. Attach the apples to the bulletin board as illustrated.
8. To create interest, use a felt-tip marker or fringed paper to add grass.

Variations
Use the bulletin board for attendance and transition activities.
Create an interactive bulletin board providing an additional set of name cards for the children to match.
Encourage the children to print their names on individual cards.
Encourage the children to create a self-portrait.

Developmental Goals

To recognize the names of other children
To develop visual discrimination skills
To develop eye-hand coordination skills
To develop a sense of community

Name the lambs.

Related Themes
Farm Animals
Animals
Nursery rhymes
Letters
Communication
Books
Names
Symbols

Alternate Titles
Lambs at School

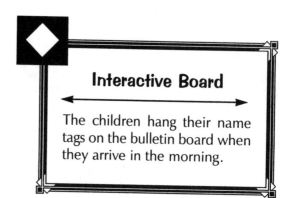

Interactive Board

The children hang their name tags on the bulletin board when they arrive in the morning.

Materials
paper or fabric for background and border.
construction paper or tagboard
pencil, markers, crayons or craypas
opaque or overhead projector, optional
scissors
hole punch
map pins or cup hooks
basket, tray or box

Preparation
1. Cover the bulletin board with construction paper, wrapping paper, shelf paper or fabric.
2. Construct a scalloped border from paper that complements the background color.
3. Trace, cut and attach letters to create the title.
4. Sketch freehand or use an opaque or overhead projector to trace one lamb for each child in the class on construction paper or tagboard.
5. Cut out the lambs from the paper.
6. Color and add details to the lambs, such as head, ears, eyes, nose, mouth and feet. Then print each child's name on a lamb.
7. Cover the lambs with clear contact paper or laminate.
8. Punch a hole in the top of the head of each lamb.
9. Attach map pins or cup hooks in rows, allowing sufficient space to hang one lamb name tag for each child in the class.
10. Put the name tags in a basket, tray or box attached to or adjacent to the bulletin board.

Variation
Adapt to use with any theme by changing the figure, such as valentines or pumpkins.

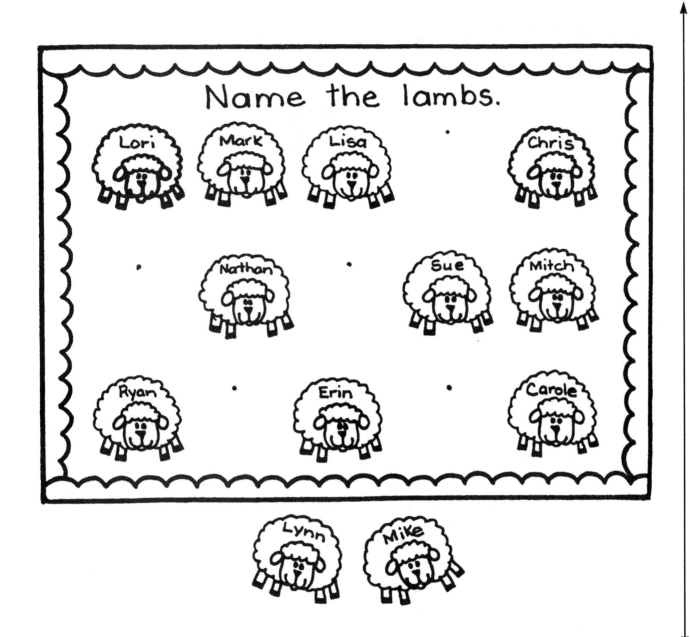

Developmental Goals

To practice identifying one's own name
To develop eye-hand coordination skills
To practice visual discrimination skills
To develop an appreciation for the printed word
To practice decoding symbols and names
To develop left-to-right progression skills

Needles and Thread

Related Themes
Crafts
Sewing
Hobbies
Colors

Alternate Title
Match the thread colors.

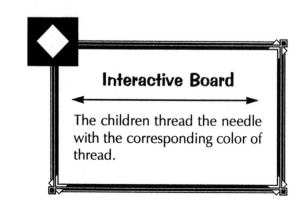

Interactive Board

The children thread the needle with the corresponding color of thread.

Materials
paper or fabric for background and border
construction paper or tagboard
pencil, markers, crayons or craypas
opaque or overhead projector, optional
scissors
blue, yellow, red, purple, orange and pink yarn

Preparation
1. Cover the bulletin board with construction paper or fabric in a color that will complement the thread spools.
2. Cut and attach a border.
3. Trace, cut and attach letters to create a title.
4. Sketch freehand or use the opaque or overhead projector to trace seven spools of thread and seven needles onto colored construction paper or tagboard. One thread spool and needle are needed in each of the following colors: blue, green, yellow, red, purple, orange and pink.
5. Cut out the spools and needles.
6. Color and add details to the spools.
7. Cut pieces of blue, green, yellow, red, purple, orange and pink yarn.
8. Attach and label the spools horizontally across the lower edge of the bulletin board as illustrated.
9. To each colored spool, attach the matching colored piece of yarn.
10. Above the spools, randomly attach the needles. The opening for the eye of each needle should be large enough to easily insert the yarn piece.

Variations
Cover the needles with aluminum foil.
Print the color words on the spools of thread.

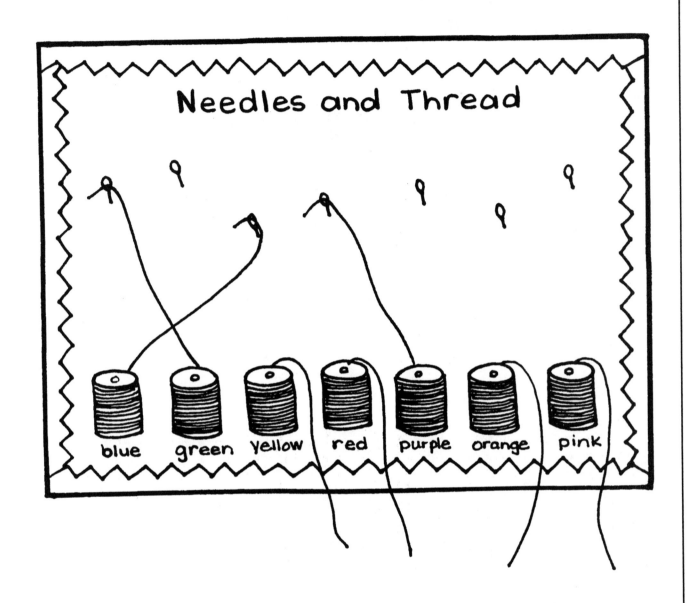

Developmental Goals

To develop visual discrimination skills

To practice eye-hand coordination skills

To associate the printed color word with the corresponding color of letters including blue, green, yellow, red, purple, orange and pink

To develop problem-solving skills

To develop small muscle coordination skills

Our Birthdays

Related Themes
Celebrations
Birthdays
Kites
Things that move

Alternate Title
Birthday Kites

Materials
paper or fabric for background and border
construction paper or tagboard
pencil, markers, crayons or craypas
opaque or overhead projector
scissors
string

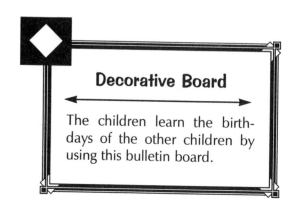

Decorative Board

The children learn the birthdays of the other children by using this bulletin board.

Preparation
1. Cover the background of the board with fabric, wrapping paper, construction paper, tagboard, wallpaper or aluminum foil.
2. Create and attach a border, if desired
3. Sketch freehand or use the overhead or opaque projector to create twelve kites and a tail for each child.
4. Cut out a cloud shape from a complementary colored paper. On the cloud print the title, "Our Birthdays." Attach the cloud to the upper left side of the board as illustrated.
5. On each kite print a different month of the year. On each tail print a child's name and his or her birth date.
6. Attach the kites to the bulletin board. To each kite attach a string and the appropriate tails with the children's name and birth dates.

Variation
Convert this bulletin board to an interactive bulletin board by preparing two sets of tails.

Developmental Goals

To recognize one's own name
To practice letter recognition
To develop visual discrimination skills
To practice decoding names of other children

Pack the suitcases.

Related Themes
Containers
Summer
Vacations
Travel

Alternate Titles
Pack your things.
Traveling
We're going on a trip.

Materials
paper or fabric for background and border
construction paper
pencil, markers, crayons or craypas
opaque or overhead projector, optional
scissors
hole punch
clear contact paper or laminate, optional
map pins or cup hooks
basket, tray or box

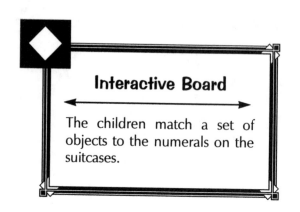

Interactive Board

The children match a set of objects to the numerals on the suitcases.

Preparation
1. Cover the bulletin board with construction paper or fabric. Add a border, created from a map if desired.
2. Trace, cut and attach letters to create the title.
3. Sketch freehand or use the opaque or overhead projector to create eight suitcases, a comb, toothbrush, toothpaste, shoes, pants, shorts, socks and shirt.
4. Cut out the suitcases and the other items.
5. Color and add details to the clothing, comb, brush, toothpaste and suitcases as illustrated. On each of the suitcases, write a numeral 1 through 8. Under each numeral on each suitcase, draw a representative number of dots.
6. Cover the suitcases and other items with clear contact paper or laminate if desired. Punch a hole in each item.
7. Attach the suitcases to the bulletin board as illustrated.
8. Attach a map pin or cup hook to each suitcase.
9. Place the clothing and personal care items in a basket, tray or box adjacent to the bulletin board.

Variations
The children can create the items to be placed in the suitcases.
Make each of the suitcases a different color and the matching colored items are placed in the
    corresponding colored suitcase.

Pack the suitcases.

Developmental Goals
To practice one-to-one correspondence
To develop numeral recognition skills
To develop visual discrimination skills
To develop problem-solving skills

Piggy Banks

Related Themes
Animals
Money
Containers

Alternate Titles
Count the money.
Money Banks
Save your money.

Materials
paper or fabric for background and border
construction paper
pencil, markers, crayons or craypas
opaque or overhead projector, optional
scissors
clear contact paper or laminate
tray or resealable plastic bag

Interactive Board
The children identify the numeral on each piggy bank and place the correct number of pennies in the slot.

Preparation
1. Cover the background with construction paper or fabric in a color that will complement the piggy banks. Add a border, if desired.
2. Trace, cut and attach letters to create the title.
3. Sketch freehand or use the opaque or overhead projector to trace six piggy banks onto colored construction paper or tagboard.
4. Cut out the piggy bank shapes.
5. Color and add the details, such as ears, eyes, nose and mouth to each piggy bank.
6. Cut opening to "deposit" coins on each piggy bank. (Make it large enough to get the pennies out, too.)
7. Cover the piggy banks with clear contact paper or laminate, leaving an opening at the top.
8. Attach the piggy banks to the board as illustrated.
9. Place a tray or resealable plastic bag containing pennies adjacent to the bulletin board.
Caution: With young children who still put things in their mouths, provide close supervision when they are working with the pennies.

Variation
Vary the number of banks and numerals according to the children's developmental levels.

Developmental Goals

To improve eye-hand coordination skills
To practice numeral recognition skills
To improve one-to-one correspondence skills
To develop problem-solving skills
To develop small muscle coordination skills
To develop visual discrimination skills

Play tic-tac-toe.

Related Themes
Games
Symbols
Rules

Alternate Titles
Can you play tic-tac-toe?
Play a game.

Materials
paper or fabric for background and border
construction paper or tagboard
scissors
clear contact paper or laminate
masking tape
resealable plastic bag

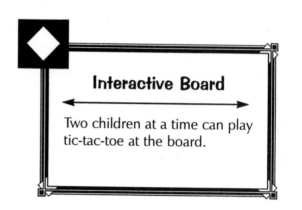

Interactive Board

Two children at a time can play tic-tac-toe at the board.

Preparation
1. Cover the background of the bulletin board with fabric, colored construction paper, wrapping paper, shelf paper or any suitable material.
2. Measure the bulletin board and cut a 3″ strip border. To create interest, using a felt-tip marker or craypa, mark Xs and Os as illustrated. Attach the border.
3. Trace, cut and attach bulletin board letters to create the title.
4. Cut four 2″x20″ strips from construction paper or tagboard.
5. Enlarge the patterns for the uppercase letters X and O. Trace them onto a contrasting colored paper and cut out.
6. Cover the Xs and Os with clear contact paper or laminate.
7. Attach the four strips as illustrated to form the grid for tic-tac-toe.
8. Attach a resealable plastic bag to the bottom of the board. Place the Xs and Os and masking tape in the bag.

Variations
Create the board using different colors.
Design symbols to complement the theme, such as shapes or holidays.

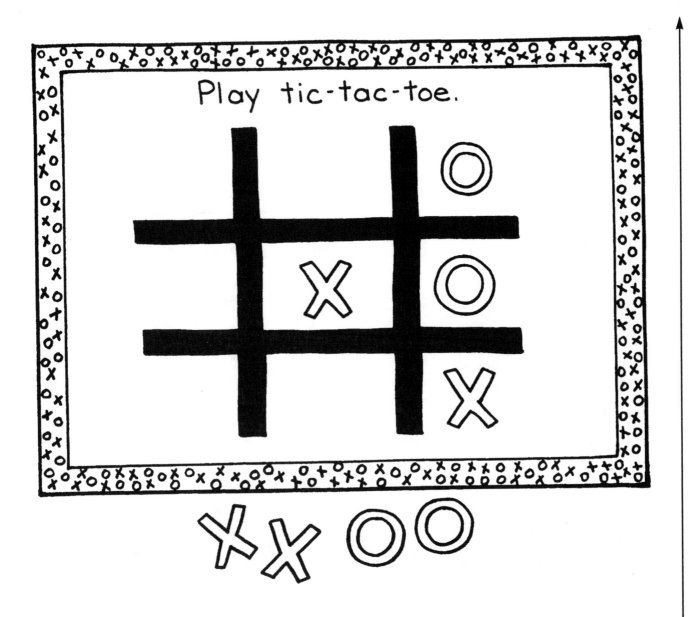

Play tic-tac-toe.

Developmental Goals

To practice eye-hand coordination skills
To recognize the shape of the letters X and O
To develop visual discrimination skills
To practice taking turns
To practice following directions

Put Humpty together.

Related Themes
Food
Nursery rhymes
Puzzles

Alternate Titles
Help Humpty Dumpty.
Humpty

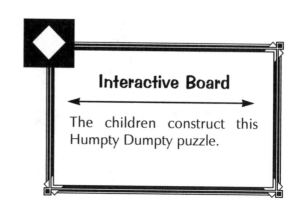

Interactive Board

The children construct this Humpty Dumpty puzzle.

Materials
paper or fabric for background or border
black and white construction paper or tagboard
pencil, markers, crayons or craypas
opaque or overhead projector, optional
scissors
clear contact paper or laminate
velcro
basket, tray or resealable plastic bag

Preparation
1. Cover the background of the bulletin board with paper or fabric. Add a border, if desired.
2. Trace, cut out and attach letters to create the title.
3. Sketch freehand or use the opaque or overhead projector to create 2 Humpty figures. One figure should be on black tagboard or construction paper to create the shadow. The other figure can be on white tagboard or construction paper.
4. Cut out Humpty and the body pieces.
5. Color and add the eyes, nose, mouth and bow tie to the white outlines of Humpty.
6. Cover Humpty and the body pieces with clear contact paper or laminate.
7. On the bottom one third of the bulletin board, draw brick shapes using a wide felt-tip marker as illustrated.
8. Attach the black colored Humpty to the bulletin board as a shadow.
9. Cut the Humpty constructed on white tagboard into shapes. Put velcro on the backs of the white pieces of Humpty and on the black shadow outlines of Humpty.
10. Put the white pieces in a basket, tray or resealable plastic bag adjacent to the bulletin board.

Variation
Vary the size of the pieces according to the developmental level of the children. For older children, prepare smaller, more intricate pieces.

Developmental Goals
To develop problem-solving skills
To practice the nursery rhyme
To improve eye-hand coordination skills
To develop problem-solving skills
To develop visual discrimination skills

Red Rectangle Robots

Related Themes
Colors
Shapes
Robots
Things that move
The letter R

Alternate Titles
Our Work
Things Made with Shapes
Rectangles

Materials
paper, tagboard or fabric
construction paper or tagboard
pencil, markers
red paper
scissors
glue

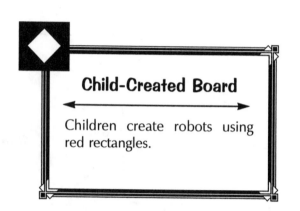

Child-Created Board
Children create robots using red rectangles.

Preparation
1. Cover the background of the bulletin board with paper, tagboard or fabric.
2. Trace, cut and attach red letters to create a title.
3. Cut 8"x12" rectangles and 2"x7" strips from construction paper or tagboard. The number of rectangles will depend on the size of the bulletin board or the number of children.
4. Provide the children with an 8"x12" rectangle, scissors, glue and precut rectangle-shaped pieces of various sizes and textures.
5. Using felt-tip markers, print the children's name on the strips.
6. Attach the children's names to their designs on the board.

Variation
For younger children, ask them to create their own designs and change the title to "Our Designs."

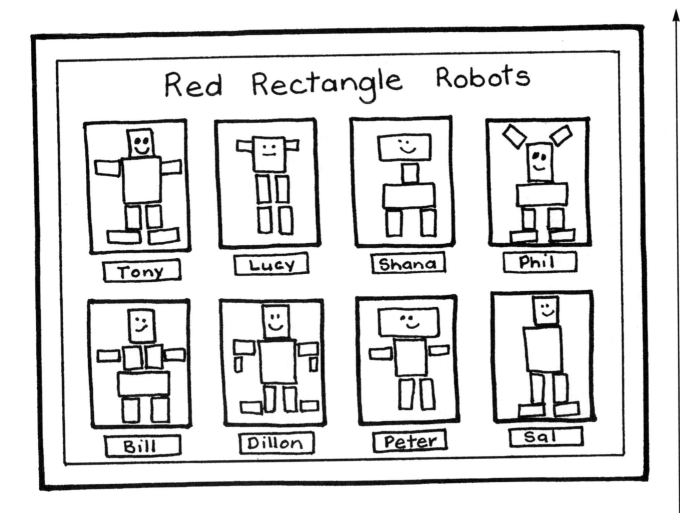

Developmental Goals

To recognize one's own name
To develop an appreciation for art forms and basic shapes
To develop creativity
To develop problem-solving skills
To develop eye-hand coordination skills
To develop visual discrimination skills

Shamrock Math

Related Themes
St. Patrick's Day
Spring
Holidays
Symbols
Numerals

Alternate Titles
Match the shamrocks.
Shamrock Fun!

Materials
paper, fabric or wrapping paper for background and border
green construction paper or tagboard
pencil, markers, crayons or craypas
opaque or overhead projector, optional
scissors
hole punch
clear contact paper or laminate
map pins or cup hooks
basket, tray or box

Interactive Board
The children match the numeral on each shamrock to the shamrock on the bulletin board that has the corresponding number of dots.

Preparation
1. Cover the background of the bulletin board with colored construction paper, fabric or wrapping paper.
2. Cut and attach a scalloped border to add interest.
3. Trace, cut and attach letters to create the title.
4. Sketch freehand or use the opaque or overhead projector to trace 24 shamrocks on green colored construction paper or tagboard.
5. Cut out the shamrocks.
6. On one set of 12 shamrocks, use a felt-tip marker to print numerals, beginning with 1 and continuing through 12 as illustrated. Punch a hole in the top of these shamrocks. On each of the shamrocks in the other set draw the number of dots that correspond with one of the numerals from 1 through 12.
7. Cover the shamrocks with clear contact paper or laminate.
8. Attach the shamrocks with dots to the bulletin board. Put a map pin or cup hook at the top of each shamrock.
9. Place the shamrocks with numerals in a basket, tray or box adjacent to the bulletin board.

Variations

Print upper and/or lower case letters on the shamrocks.
Adapt this board to use with other themes, such as Valentine's Day, Thanksgiving, Easter, Hannukah, Halloween, Christmas.

Developmental Goals

To match numerals to a corresponding set
To develop one-to-one correspondence skills
To develop visual discrimination skills
To develop small muscle coordination skills
To develop problem-solving skills
To practice decoding symbols

Sing a song of sixpence.

Related Themes
Our school birds
Nursery rhymes
Friends
Music

Alternate Titles
Our Class
Blackbirds
Who was in the pie?

Interactive Board

The children hang their black-bird name tags on the bulletin board when they arrive at the center or school.

Materials
paper for the background and border
construction paper
pencil, markers, crayons or craypas
opaque or overhead projector, optional
scissors
hole punch
map pins or cup hooks
basket, tray or box

Preparation
1. Cover the background of the bulletin board with paper that will complement the bulletin board design. Add a border, if desired.
2. Trace, cut and attach letters to create the title.
3. Sketch freehand or use an opaque or overhead projector to trace a bird for each child in the class and one large pie onto colored construction paper.
4. Cut out the pie and the birds. Using a hole punch, make a hole in the top of each bird.
5. Color and add details to the pie as well as eyes and beaks to the birds. Then print each child's name on a bird.
6. Attach the pie to the bulletin board as illustrated.
7. Add map pins or cup hooks randomly to the board, providing one pin or hook for each child.
8. Place the birds in a basket, tray or box adjacent to the bulletin board.

Variation
Use the board to call attention to each child's name during group activity time.

Sing a song of sixpence.

Developmental Goals
To practice identifying the letters in one's own name
To develop an appreciation of nursery rhymes
To explore a print rich environment
To recognize other children's names
To develop visual discrimination skills
To develop problem-solving skills
To practice following directions

Sort the gum balls.

Related Themes
Color
Candy
Containers

Alternate Titles
Gum Ball Sort
Colored Gum Balls

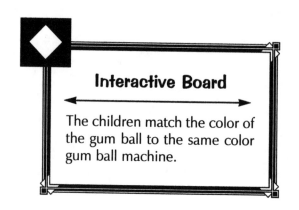

Interactive Board

The children match the color of the gum ball to the same color gum ball machine.

Materials
paper or fabric for background and border
colored tagboard
pencil, markers, crayons or craypas
opaque or overhead projector, optional
scissors
clear contact paper or laminate, optional
velcro
basket, tray or box

Preparation
1. Cover the background of the bulletin board with paper or fabric.
2. Cut and attach a border.
3. Trace, cut and attach letters to create a title.
4. Sketch freehand or use an overhead or opaque projector to trace the gum ball machines and gum balls. Use red, blue, yellow, green, purple, orange, pink, white and black for the gum balls and the gum ball machines.
5. Cut out the gum ball machines.
6. If desired, cover the pieces with clear contact paper or laminate.
7. Label and attach the gum ball machines as illustrated.
8. Attach a 1/4" strip of velcro to the front of the gum ball machines and to the backs of the gum balls.
9. Place the gum balls in a small basket, tray or box adjacent to the bulletin board.

Variation
Print numerals, instead of colors, on each gum ball machine.

Sort the gum balls.

Developmental Goals

To practice color recognition skills
To develop eye-hand coordination skills
To develop visual recognition skills
To develop problem-solving skills
To practice decoding printed words

Take note of the songs we know!

Related Themes
Music
Creativity
Nursery rhymes
Rhythm and movement

Alternate Titles
Our Songs
Sing with us.

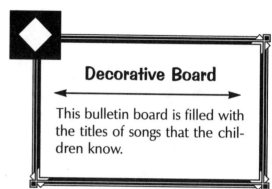

Decorative Board

This bulletin board is filled with the titles of songs that the children know.

Materials
paper, tagboard or fabric for background and border
construction paper
pencil, markers, crayons or craypas
opaque or overhead projector, optional
scissors
clear contact paper or laminate, optional

Preparation
1. Cover the background of the bulletin board with colored paper or fabric.
2. Cut a 2" border from tagboard. To create interest, decorate the border with musical notes. Attach the border.
3. Trace, cut and attach letters to create a title.
4. Sketch freehand or use an opaque or overhead projector to create a musical note for each of the children's favorite songs.
5. Cut out the notes.
6. Using a felt-tip marker, print a song title on each of the notes.
7. If desired, cover the notes with clear contact paper or laminate.
8. Attach the musical notes in an interesting pattern.

Variations
Create an interactive bulletin board by making a second set of notes to match the first set.
Add additional notes as the children learn new songs.

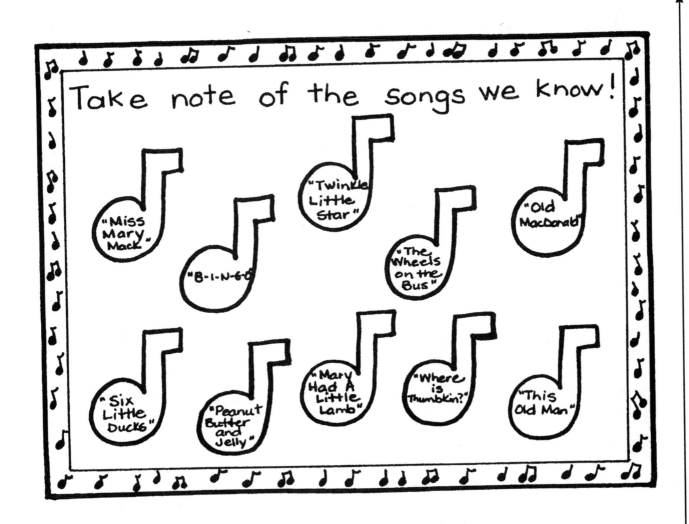

Developmental Goals

To practice decoding written words
To practice letter and word recognition
To develop visual discrimination skills

The Toy Store

Related Themes
Gifts
Holidays
Toys

Alternate Titles
Shopping for Toys
Toys

Materials
paper or fabric for background
construction paper or tagboard
pencil, markers, crayons or craypas
opaque or overhead projector, optional
scissors
masking tape
basket, tray or box

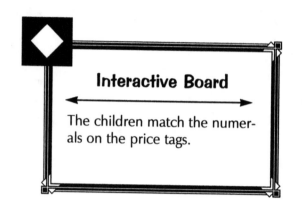

Interactive Board
The children match the numerals on the price tags.

Preparation
1. Cover the background of the board with colored paper or fabric.
2. Trace, cut and attach letters to create the title.
3. Sketch freehand or use the opaque or overhead projector to trace the awning, 12 outlines of toys and 12 price tags on colored tagboard or construction paper. The toys should be familiar to the children, such as a block, train, teddy bear, doll, ball and top.
4. Cut out the toys and price tags.
5. Color and add details to the awning and toys as illustrated.
6. Attach the awning and toys.
7. On one set of price tags record the prices and attach them to the toys on the bulletin board. Make an identical set of price tags.
8. Place the second set of price tags and masking tape in a tray, box or basket and place adjacent to the bulletin board.

Variation
Leave the tags blank and encourage the children to price the items, if developmentally appropriate.

Developmental Goals

To identify numerals
To develop visual discrimination skills
To develop problem-solving skills
To develop eye-hand coordination skills
To practice decoding symbols

Traffic Light

Related Themes
Safety
Colors
Communication
Signs
Writing
Writing tools

Alternate Titles
Safety Sign
Safety Colors

Materials
paper or fabric for background and border
tagboard
construction paper
scissors
paste or glue
markers
clear contact paper or laminate
grease pencils
piece of felt
resealable plastic bag

Interactive Board
The children practice writing the color words "red," "yellow" and "green" and match the color words to the corresponding colors on the bulletin board.

Preparation
1. Cover the background of the bulletin board with paper or fabric.
2. Cut and attach a scalloped border to add interest.
3. Trace, cut and attach letters to create the title.
4. Cut a 5"x16" rectangle and three 4"x8" rectangles from tagboard.
5. Trace a round saucer shape onto a piece of green, red and yellow construction paper. Cut out the circles.
6. Paste the red circle at the top of the 5"x16" rectangle to resemble a traffic light. Then attach the yellow shape and the green shape.
7. If developmentally appropriate, on one of the 4"x8" rectangles print the word "yellow." Under each word print the word again using broken lines. Repeat using green on a rectangle and red on another rectangle. Cover with clear contact paper or laminate.
8. Attach the traffic light to the left side of the bulletin board. Attach the rectangles containing the three color words to the right side as illustrated.
9. Place several grease pencils and a piece of felt to wipe off the marks in a resealable plastic bag. Attach to the bulletin board.

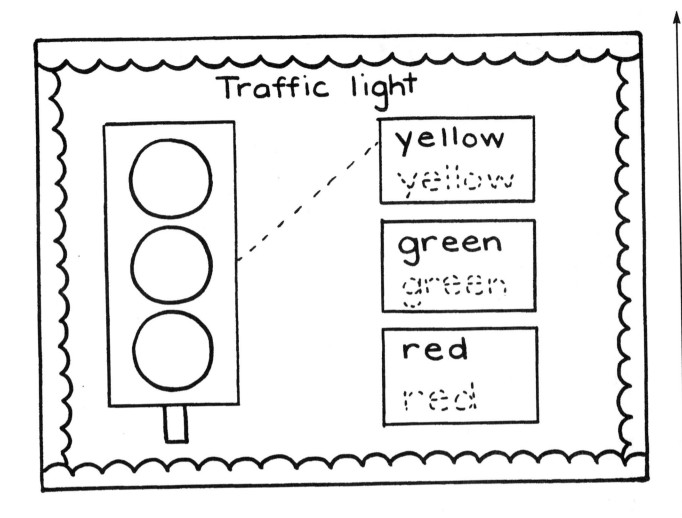

Traffic light

Variation
Omit the color words.

Developmental Goals
To identify color words
To match color words to the corresponding colors
To develop an appreciation for the printed word
To practice forming letters
To develop small muscle coordination skills
To develop problem-solving skills
To develop eye-hand coordination skills

We are "batty" over books.

Related Themes
Books
Literature
Storytelling
Halloween
Animals

Alternate Titles
We love to read.
Reading is fun.
Book Bats

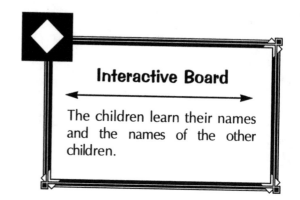

Interactive Board
The children learn their names and the names of the other children.

Materials
paper or fabric for background and border
construction paper or tagboard
marker, crayons or craypas
opaque or overhead projector, optional
scissors
map pins or cup hooks
basket, tray or box

Preparation
1. Cover the background of the bulletin board with colored paper or fabric.
2. Create and attach a scalloped border.
3. Trace, cut and attach letters to create a title.
4. Sketch freehand or use the opaque or overhead projector to create bats and a book on colored construction paper or tagboard. Create twice as many bats as the number of children.
5. Cut out the bats and the book.
6. Using felt-tip markers, print a child's name on each of two bats and add details, if desired, to the book.
7. Center and attach the book to the bulletin board. Around the book, as illustrated, attach one set of bats. Put a map pin or cup hook at the top of each name.
8. Punch holes in the second set.
9. Put this second set in a basket, tray or box adjacent to the bulletin board.

Variation
Change the title to "Favorite Books" and print the name of a book on each bat.

Developmental Goals

To recognize one's own name
To recognize other children's names
To develop an appreciation of reading
To develop visual discrimination skills

We are sailing into learning!

Related Themes
Boats
Transportation
Water

Alternate Titles
Our Class
My Friends

Materials
paper or fabric for background
construction paper or tagboard
pencil, markers, crayons or craypas
opaque or overhead projector, optional
scissors

Decorative Board

The children learn letter recognition and other children's names with this bulletin board.

Preparation
1. Cover the background of the bulletin board with fabric, wrapping paper or construction paper.
2. Sketch freehand or use a projector to draw a boat for each child on construction paper or tagboard.
3. Cut out the shapes.
4. Use a felt-tip marker, if desired, to outline the shapes.
5. Print a child's' name on each of the boats.
6. Cut out a cloud, as illustrated, from white construction paper or tagboard.
7. Print the title on the cloud.
8. Attach the cloud containing the title and each of the boats.

Variations
Create an interactive bulletin board by preparing a second set of boats for the children to match.
If developmentally appropriate, let the children print their own name.
Create a bulletin board entitled "Colored Boats." Cut the boats from different colors of paper.
   Print the color on each boat.

Developmental Goals

To recognize one's own name
To practice decoding the names of other children
To practice letter recognition
To develop visual discrimination skills

Wear a mask.

Related Themes
All about me
Costumes
Halloween
Holidays
Symbols

Alternate Titles
Fun with Masks
Disguises

Interactive Board
The children experiment trying on the various masks and observing themselves in front of a mirror.

Materials
fabric or paper for background and border
construction paper or tagboard
pencil, markers, crayons or craypas
opaque or overhead projector, optional
scissors
hole punch
clear contact paper or laminate
mirror
string or yarn, optional
map pins or cup hooks

Preparation
1. Cover the background of the board with fabric or paper to complement the masks.
2. Cut and attach a scalloped border.
3. Trace, cut and attach letters to create the title.
4. Sketch freehand or use the opaque or overhead projector to create the masks on construction paper or tagboard.
5. Cut out the masks and punch a hole on the top of each.
6. Color and add facial features and other details as illustrated.
7. Cover the masks with clear contact paper or laminate.
8. Hang a mirror in the middle of the board.
9. Hang the masks on map pins or cup hooks.

Variations
Encourage the children to create masks to hang on the board.
Hang various commercial masks on the board.
Stimulate the children's creativity by using a variety of materials to create masks. Use tin foil, feathers, pipe cleaners, yarn, fabric, cotton balls, glitter and sequins in creating masks.
Place the bulletin board near the dramatic play area of the classroom.

Developmental Goals

To experiment wearing different masks
To express oneself wearing a mask
To develop an understanding of the purposes of masks
To develop language skills
To develop visual discrimination skills

We're on the road to success.

Related Themes
Cars
Transportation
Wheels

Alternate Titles
Driving
Our Cars

Materials
paper or fabric for background and border
construction paper or tagboard
pencil, markers, crayons or craypas
opaque or overhead projector, optional
scissors
clear contact paper or laminate, optional

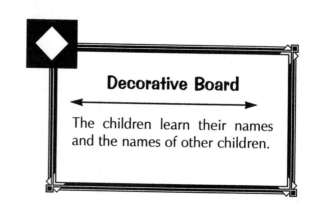

Decorative Board

The children learn their names and the names of other children.

Preparation
1. Attach a background of paper or fabric to the bulletin board. Add a border if desired.
2. Trace, cut and attach letters to create a title.
3. Sketch freehand or use an opaque or overhead projector to create cars, a roadway, sun and clouds on colored construction paper or tagboard.
4. Cut out the cars and the road.
5. Color and add details to the cars as illustrated or desired. Write one child's name on each car.
6. If desired, cover the cars with clear contact paper or laminate.
7. Attach all of the cars to the bulletin board.

Variations
Create the board using trucks or utility vehicles.
Cut the cars from different colors of construction paper and print the name of the color on each.

Developmental Goals

To recognize one's own name
To practice decoding the names of other children
To practice letter recognition
To develop visual discrimination skills

What a colorful class!

Related Themes
Colors
Writing tools
Names
Our school
Friends
School friends

Alternate Titles
Colors
My Friends at School

Materials
tagboard, fabric or paper
   for background and border
construction paper or tagboard
pencil, markers, crayons or craypas
opaque or overhead projector, optional
scissors
clear contact paper or laminate, optional
map pins or cup hooks
hole punch
basket, tray or box

Interactive Board
The children learn their names and the names of other children.

Preparation
1. Cover the background of the bulletin board with tagboard, fabric or paper.
2. Create and attach a scalloped border.
3. Trace, cut and attach letters to create the title.
4. Sketch freehand or use the opaque or overhead projector to create a set of crayons, two for each child in the class, and a crayon box.
5. Cut out the crayons and crayon box.
6. Color and add details to the crayons and crayon box. Also, print a child's name on each of two crayons.
7. If desired, cover the crayons and crayon box with clear contact paper or laminate.
8. Attach one set of the crayons and the box to the bulletin board. Put a map pin or cup hook above each crayon.
9. Punch a hole in the second set of crayons.
10. Put this second set in a basket, tray or box adjacent to the bulletin board.

Variation
If developmentally appropriate, each child can print his or her name.

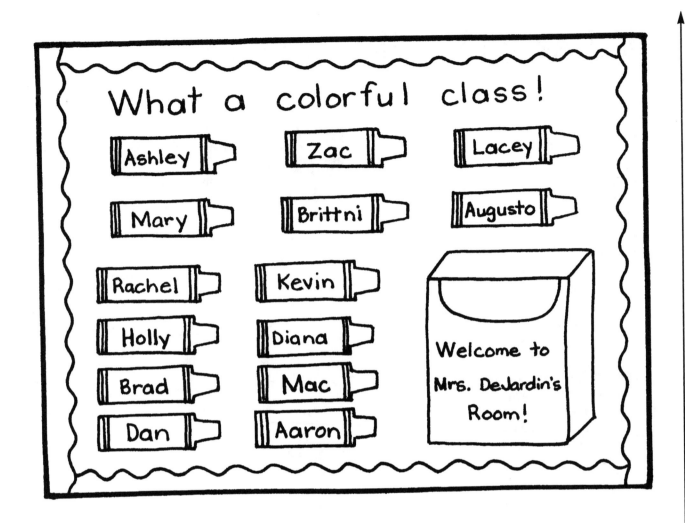

Developmental Goals

To recognize one's own name
To practice decoding the names of other children
To practice letter recognition
To develop visual discrimination skills

What will it be?

Related Themes
Numbers
Shapes
Math
Communication

Alternate Titles
Dot to Dot
Shapes

Materials
construction paper or fabric for background
pencil
opaque or overhead projector, optional
markers or grease pencils
clear contact paper or laminate
resealable plastic bag
piece of felt

Interactive Board

The children use watercolor markers or grease pencils to connect the numerals or letters sequentially, creating a shape or outline.

Preparation
1. Cover the background of the board with construction paper or fabric.
2. With a soft lead pencil sketch freehand onto the board or use an opaque or overhead projector to create the shapes of the bus, stop light and a cloud as illustrated.
3. Using a black felt-tip marker, create dots around the shapes. If developmentally appropriate for the children, add numerals to the dots.
4. Cover with clear contact paper or laminate.
5. Trace, cut and attach letters to create the title.
6. Attach a resealable plastic bag to the bulletin board. Put two grease pencils or two watercolor markers and a piece of felt to wipe off the markings in the bag.

Variations
Use letters instead of numerals.
Create more complex outlines.
Relate the shapes to a theme or holiday.

What will it be?

Developmental Goals
To develop small muscle coordination skills
To develop numeral recognition skills
To develop eye-hand coordination skills
To develop prediction skills
To develop problem-solving skills

Patterns for Name Tags and Labels

Apples

Art

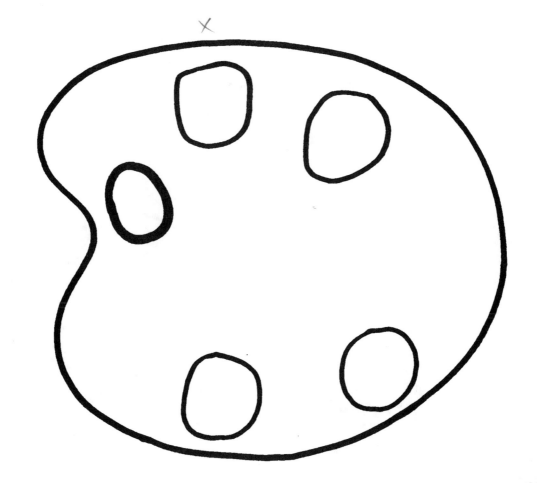

Birds

Blue

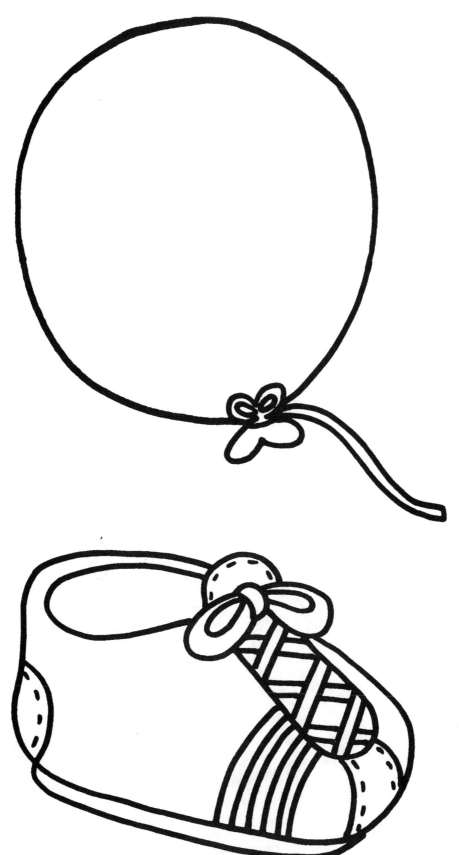

Breads

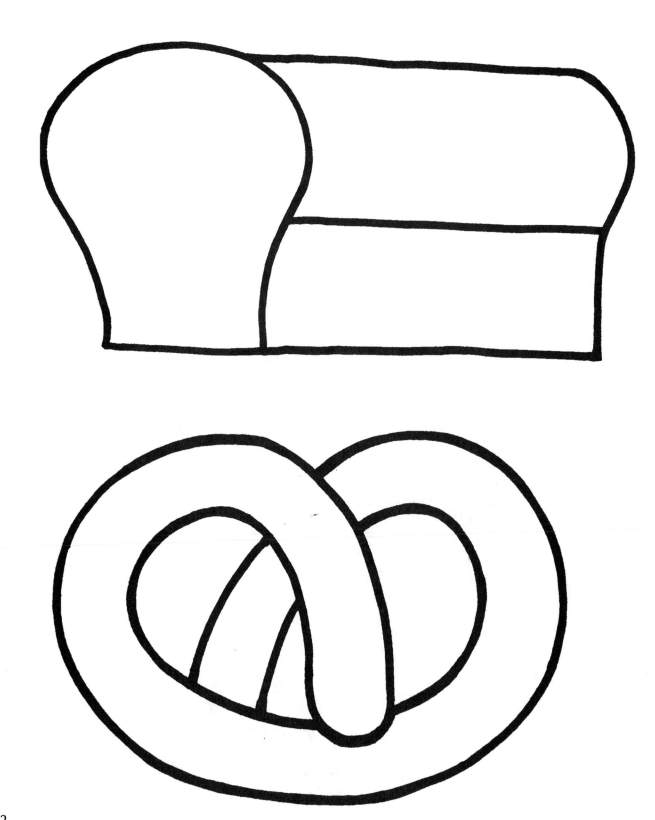

Brushes

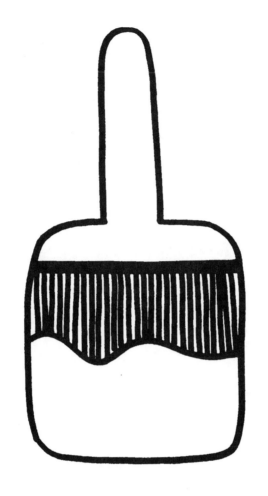

Bubbles

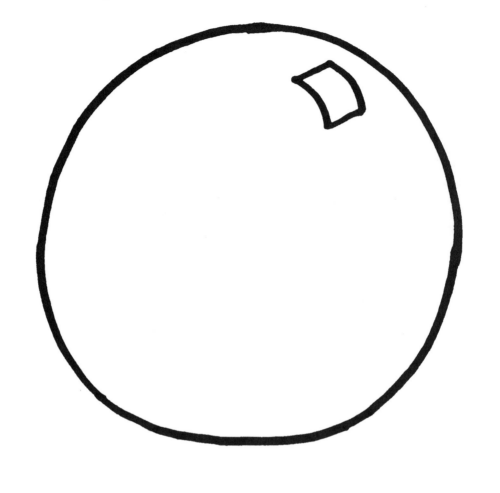

Buildings

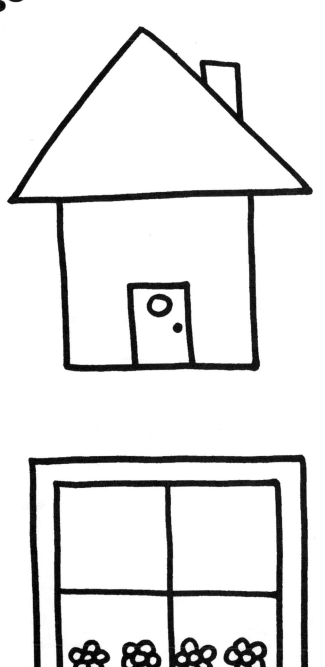

Camping

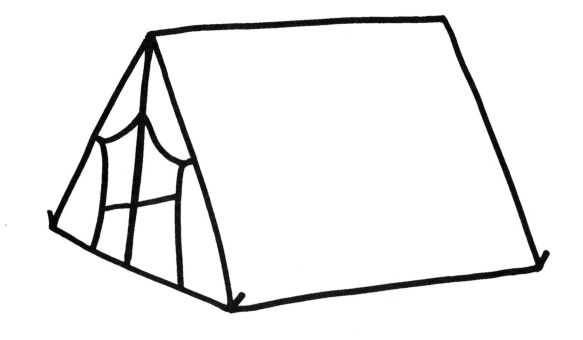

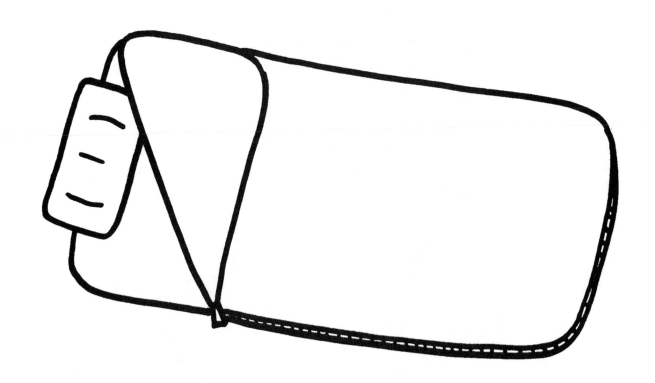

Cars, Trucks & Buses

Cats

Christmas

139

Circus

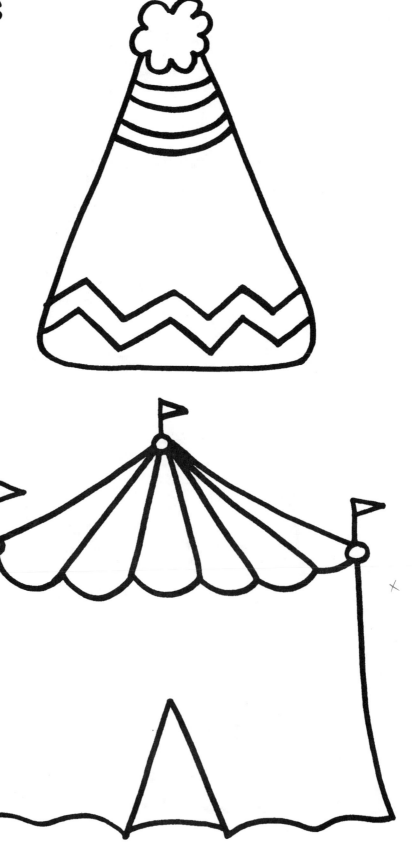

Clothes

Communication

Construction Tools

Dairy Products

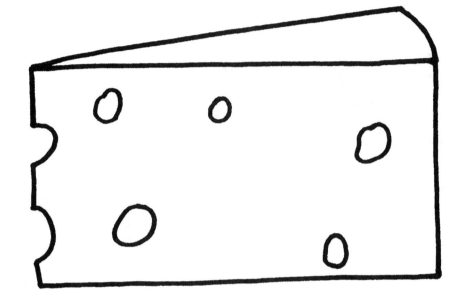

Dentist

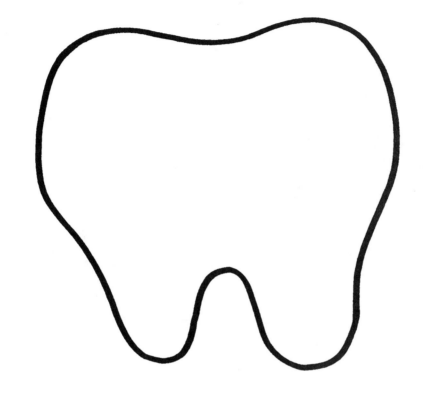

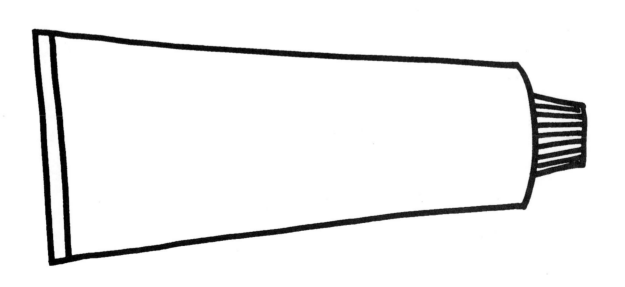

Doctors and Nurses

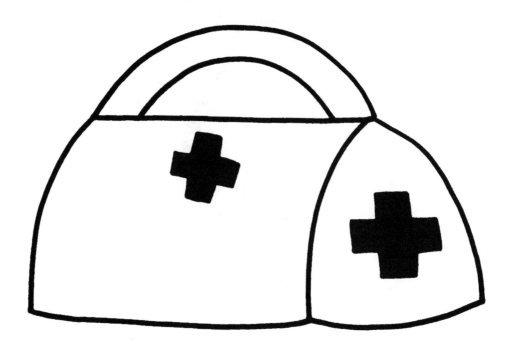

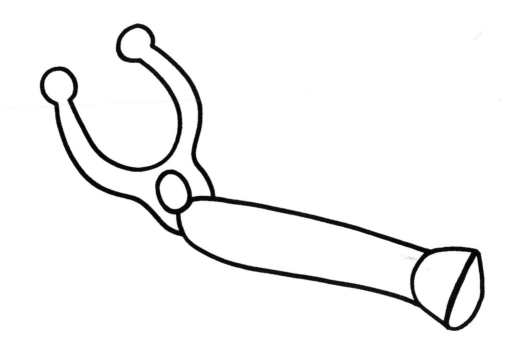

Dogs

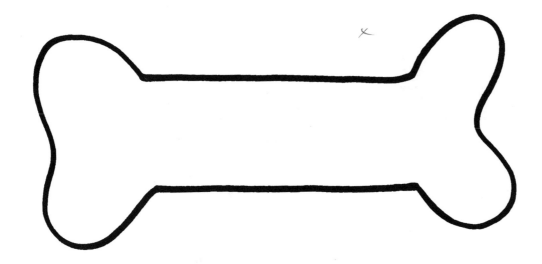

Easter

Fall

Families

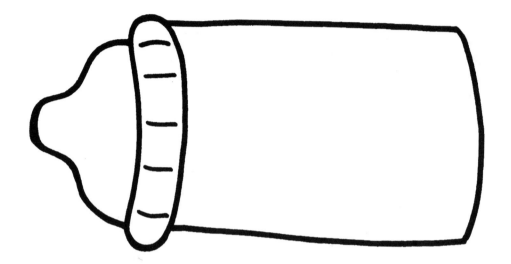

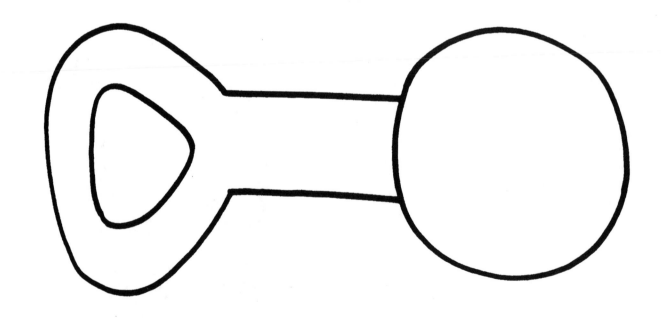

150

Farm Animals

Feelings

Firefighters

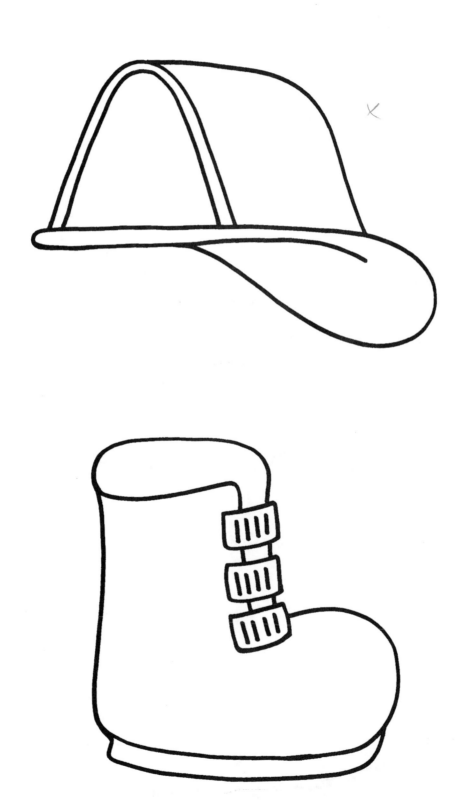

Fish

154

Flowers

Friends

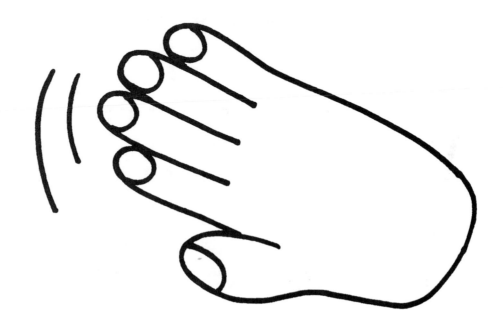

Fruits and Vegetables

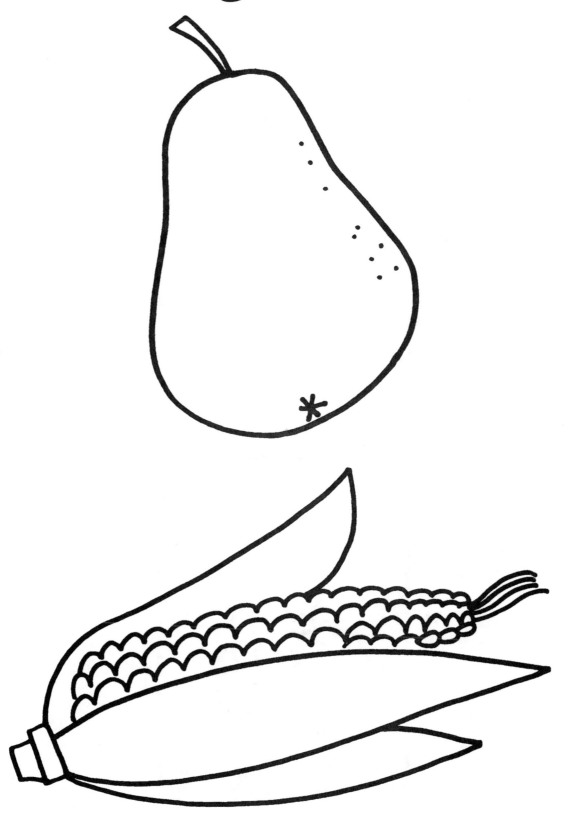

Gardens

lettuce seeds

Halloween

Hanukkah

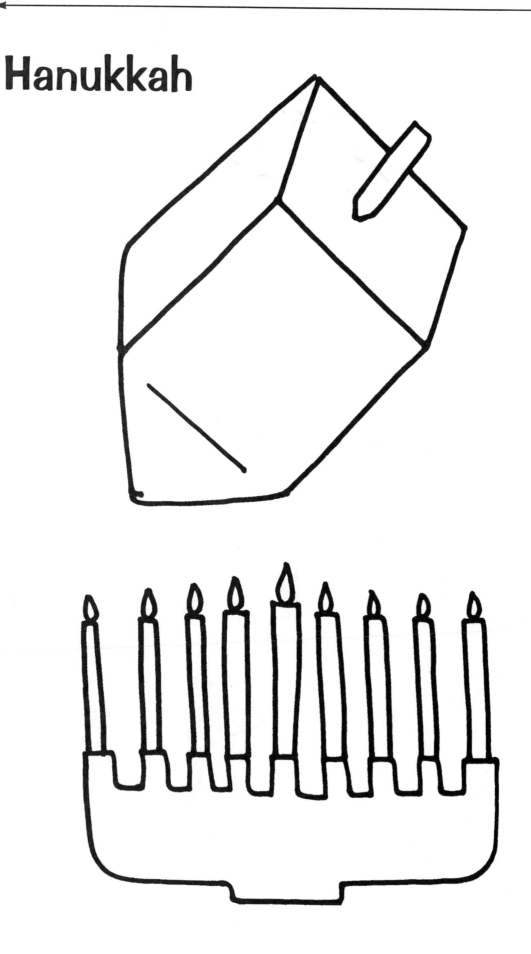

Hats

Health

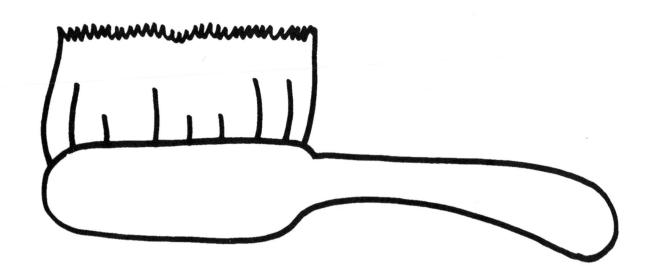

Homes

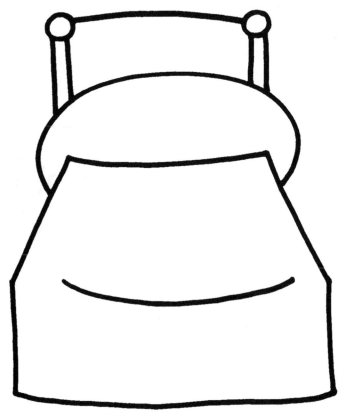

Insects and Spiders

Mail Carrier

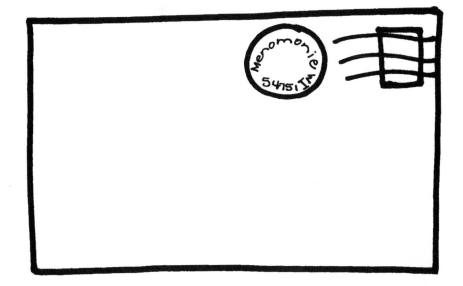

Mice

Music

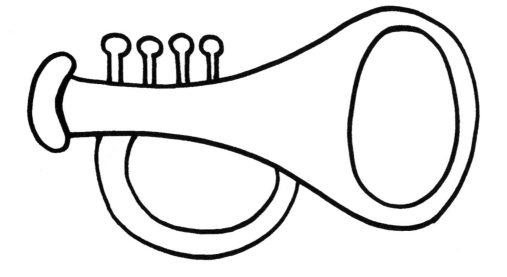

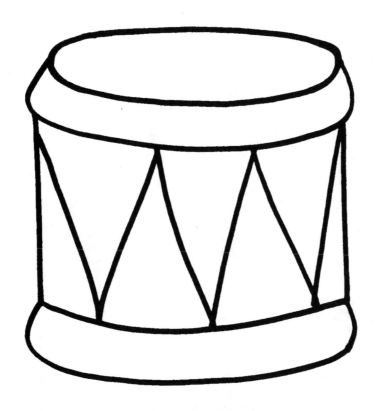

Numbers

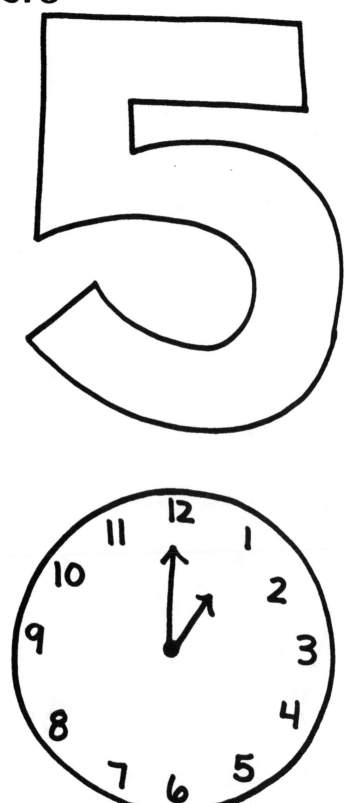

Nursery Rhymes

Pets

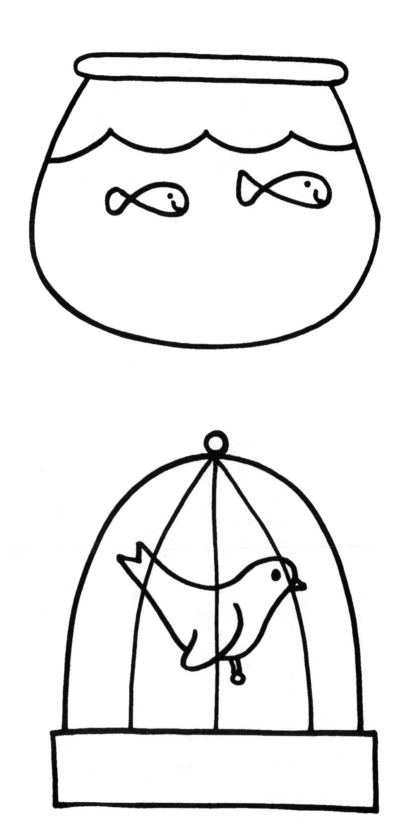

Plants

Puppets

Rain

Red

Safety

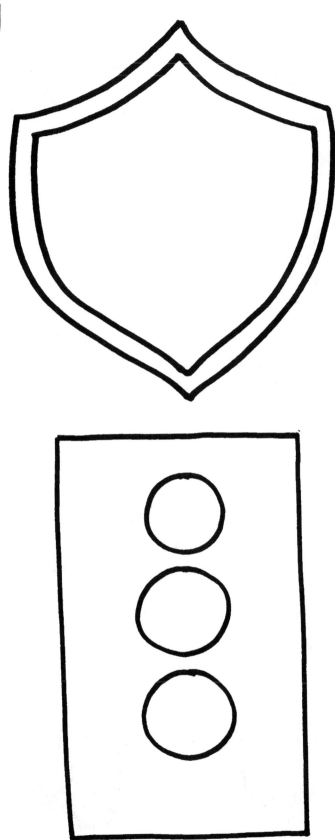

175

Shapes

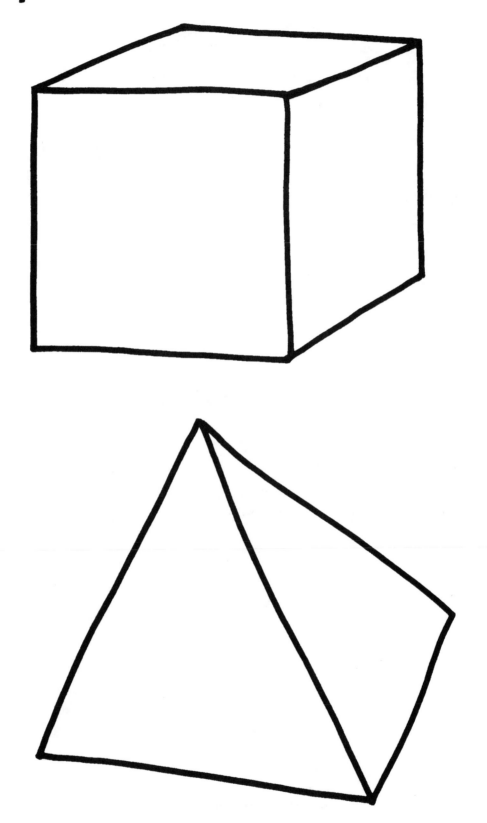

Sports

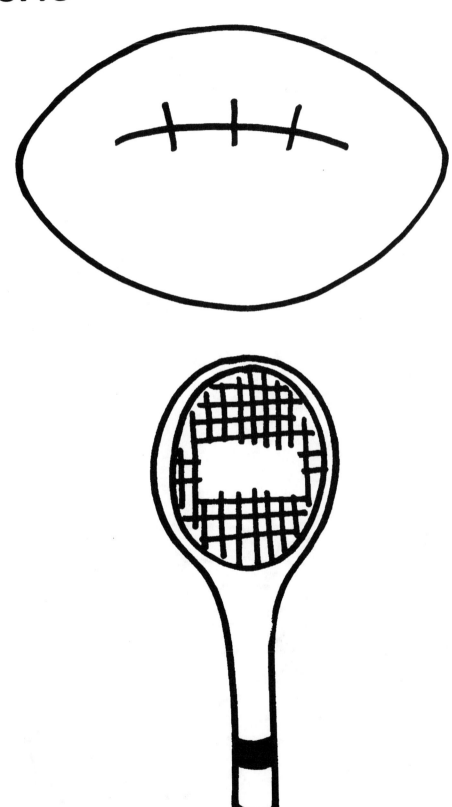

Spring

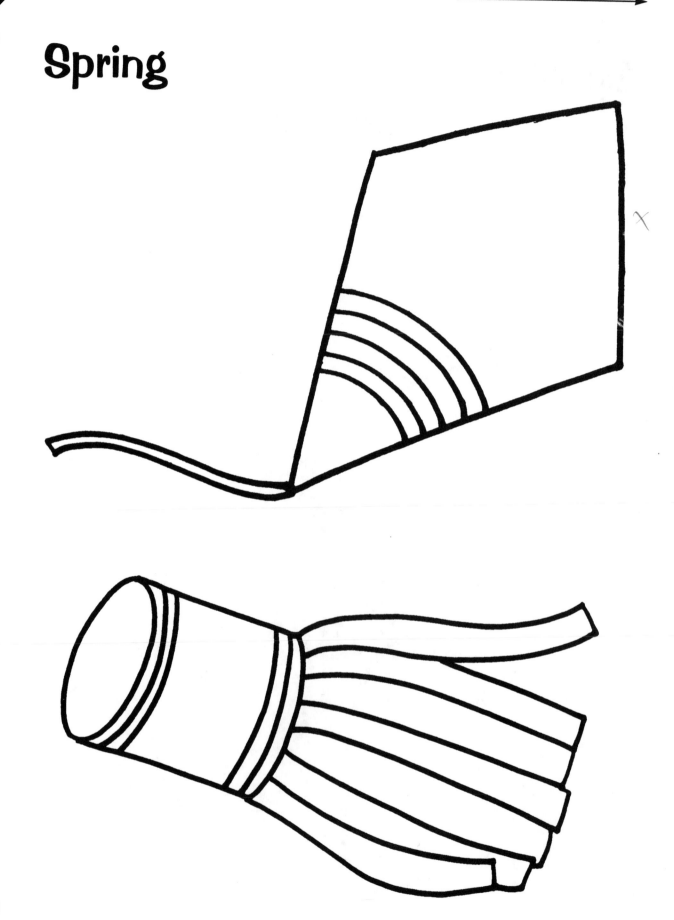

178

Summer

Thanksgiving

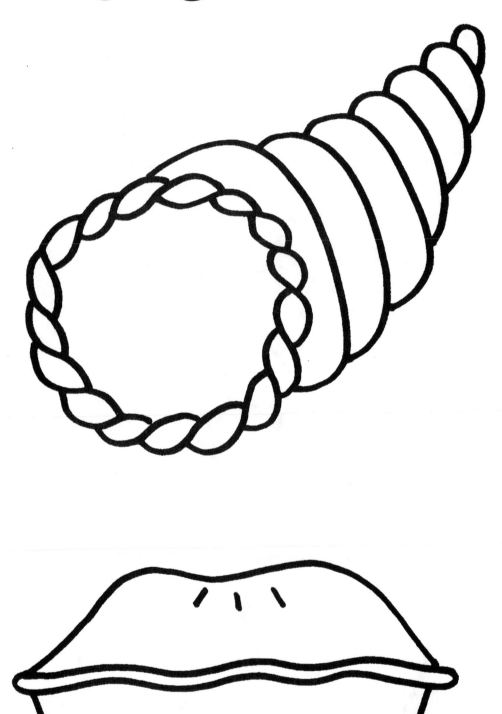

Trees

Valentine's Day

Water

Wheels

Winter

Yellow

Zoo Animals

Patterns for Letters
and Numerals

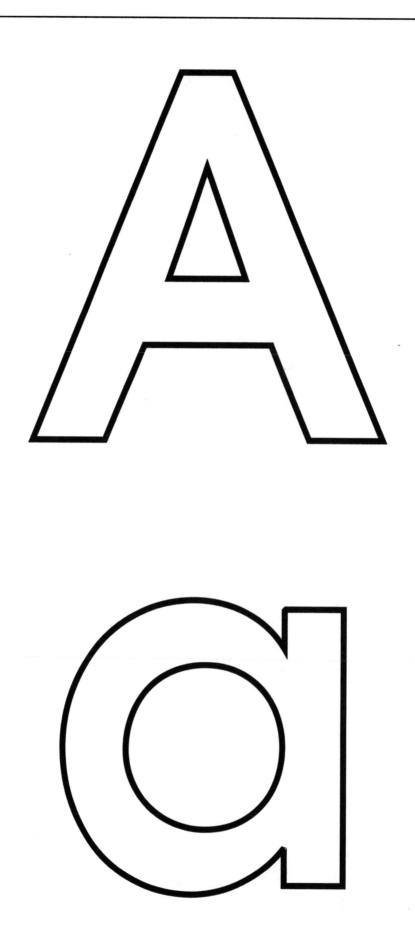

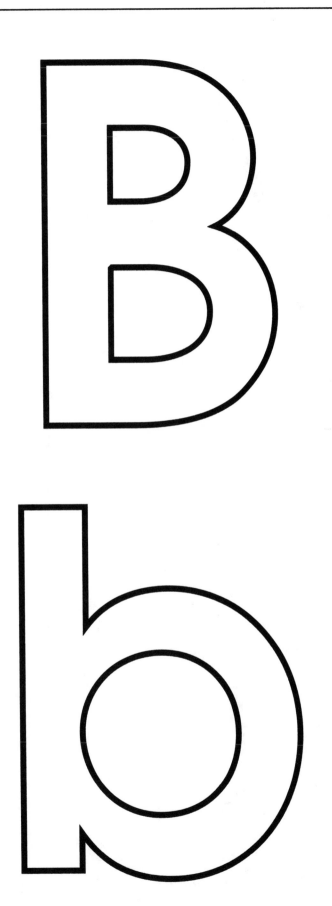

191

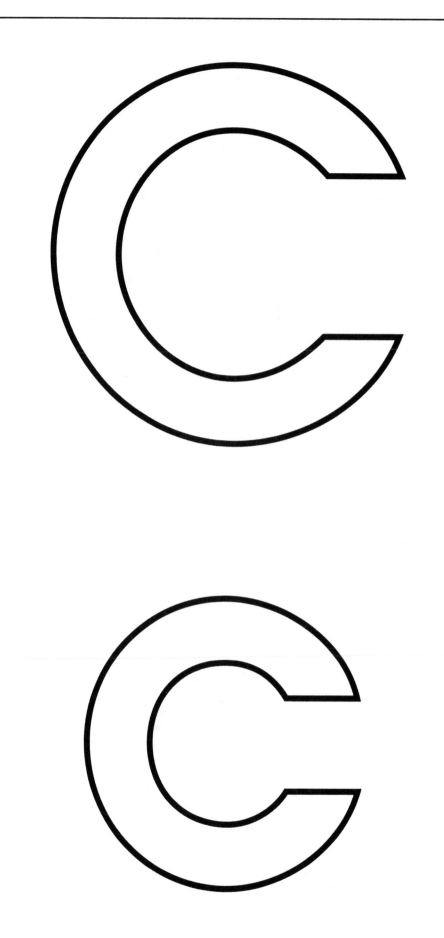

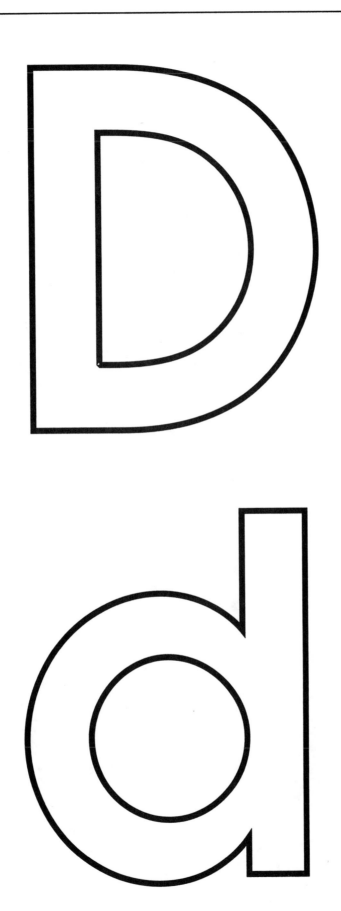

193

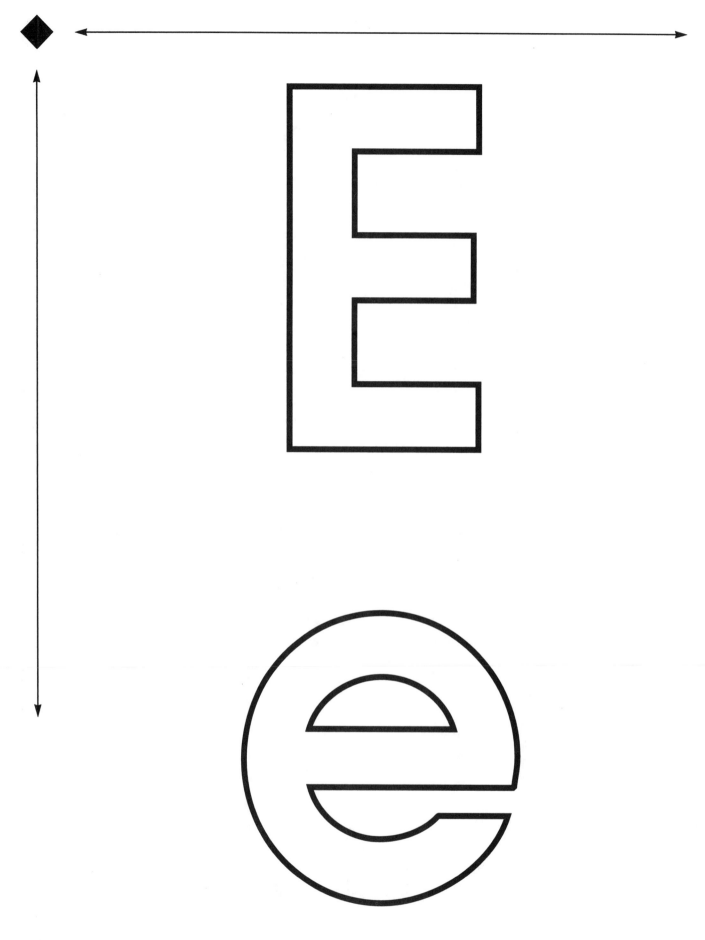

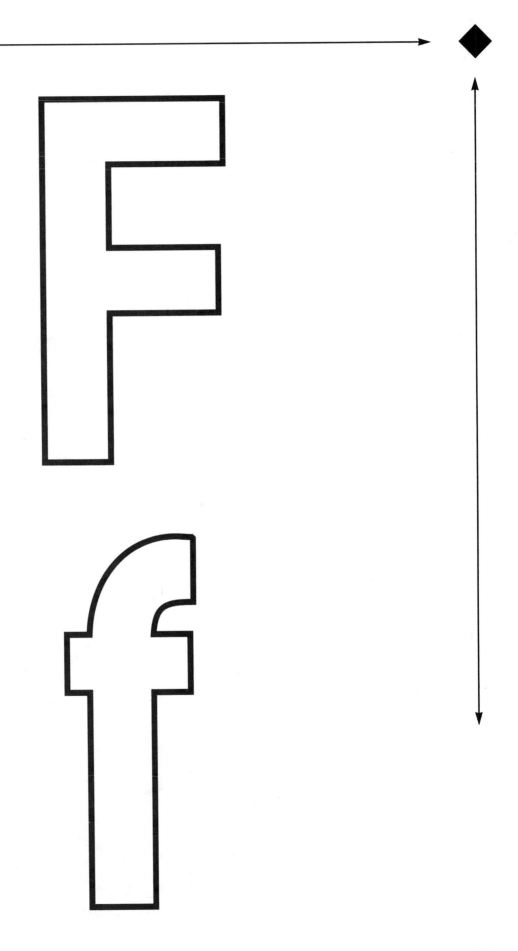

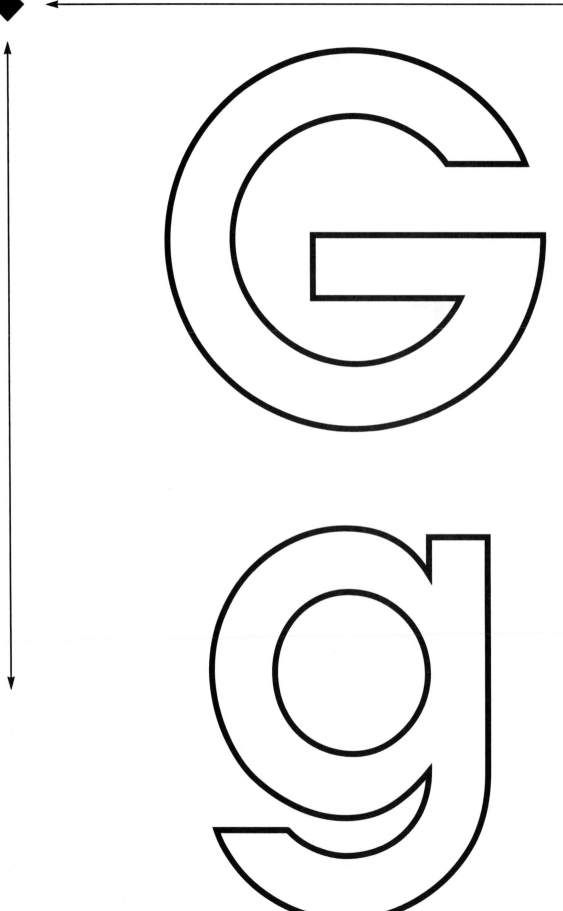

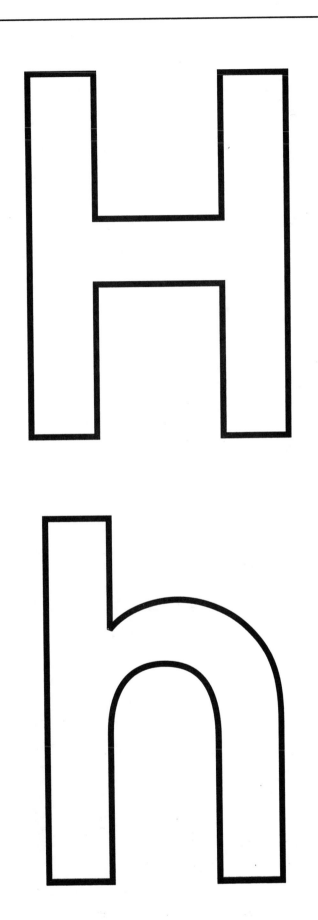

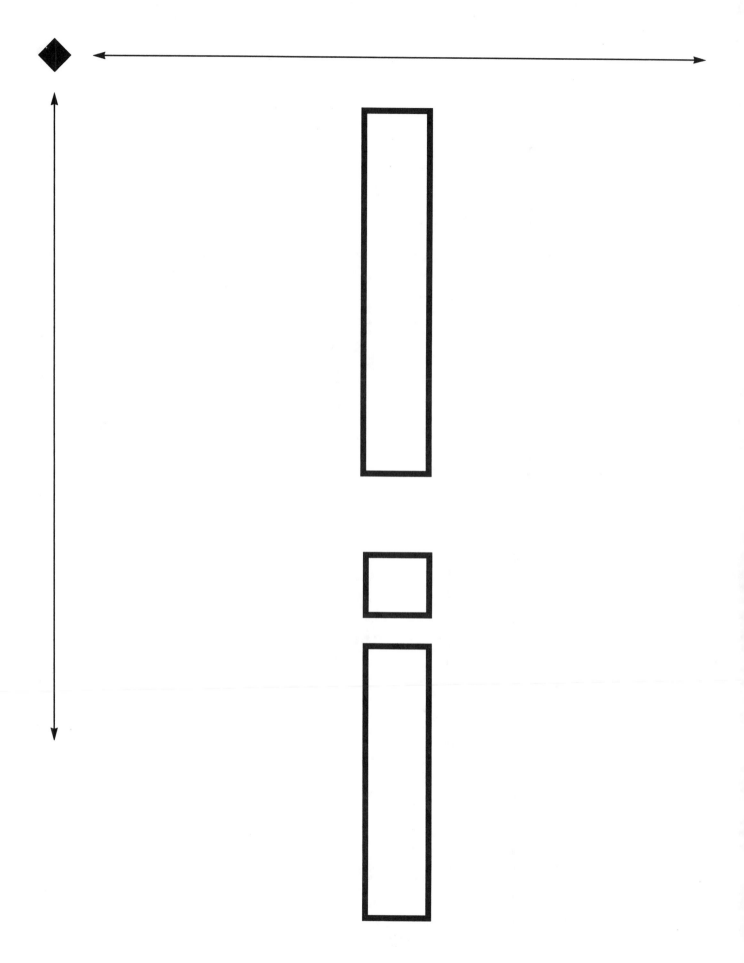

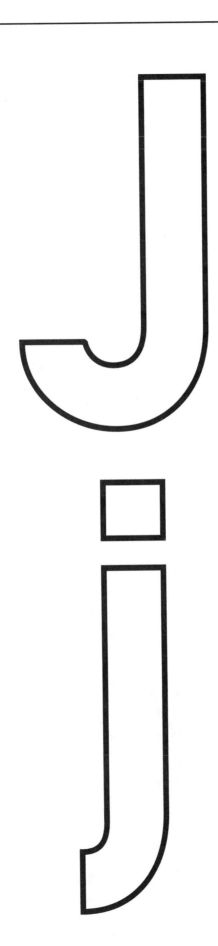

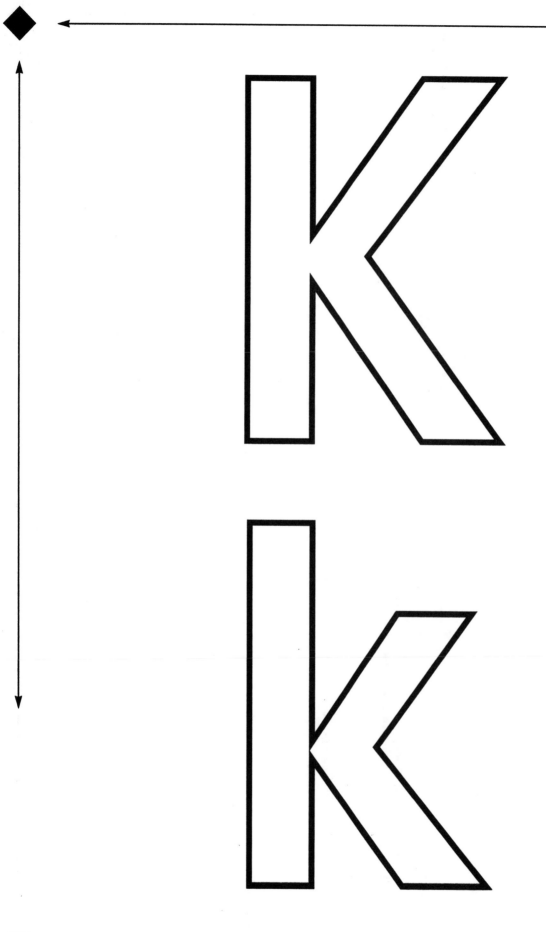

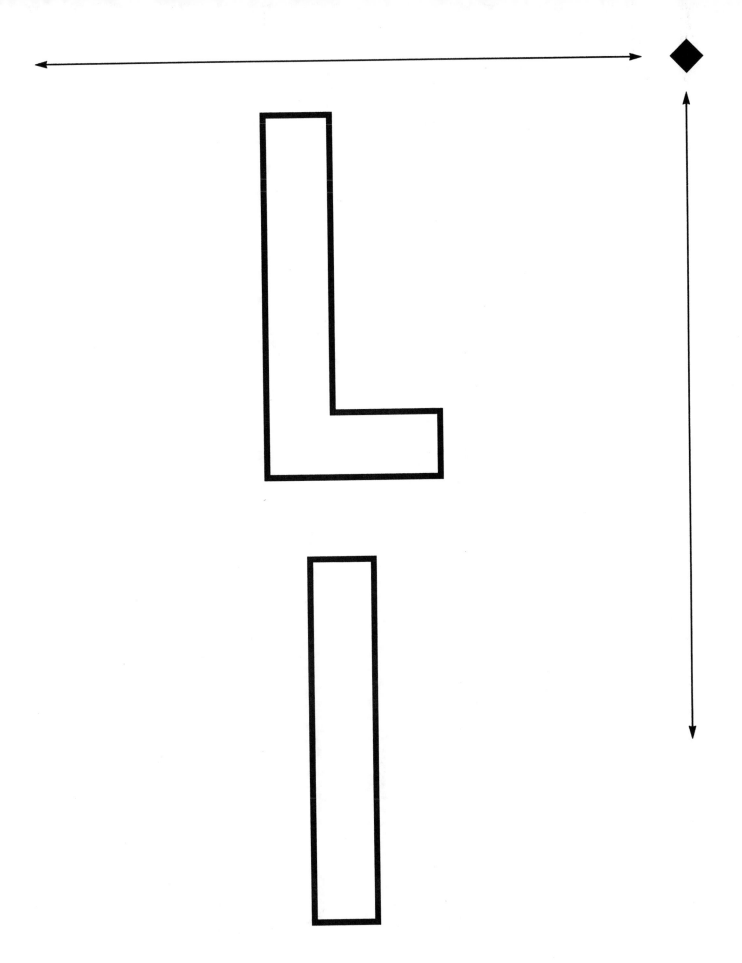

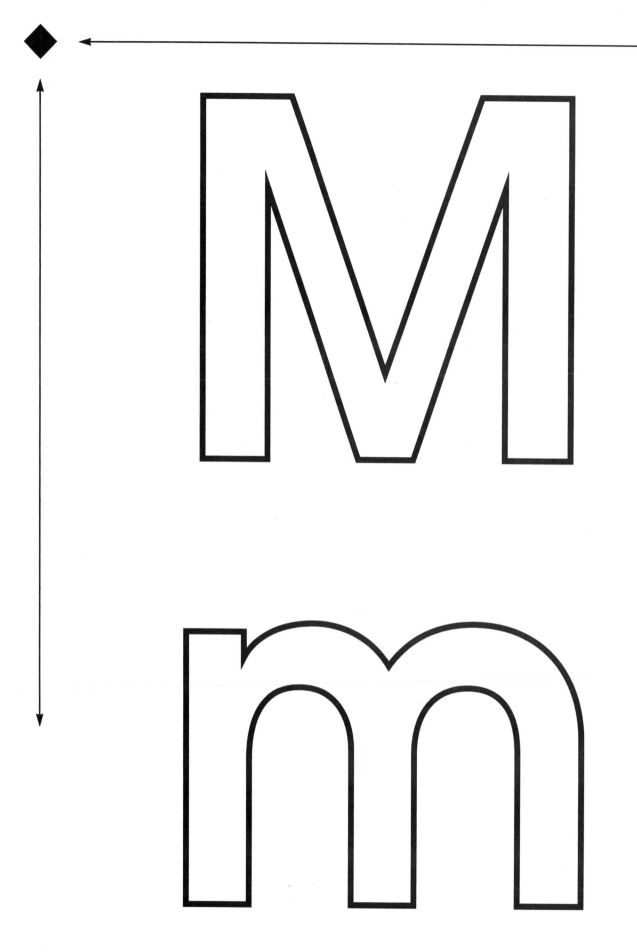

202

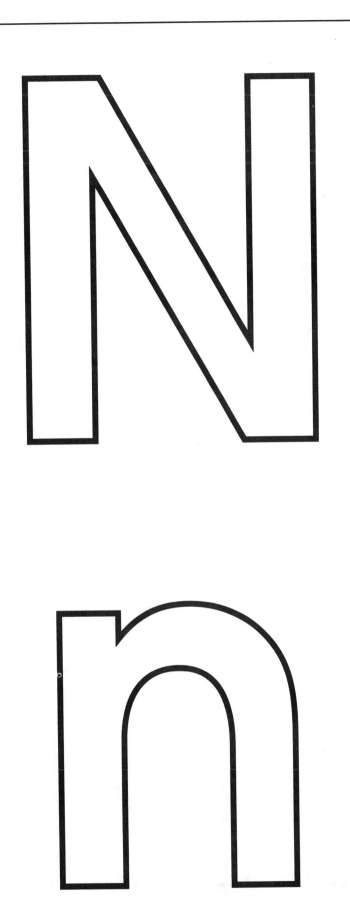

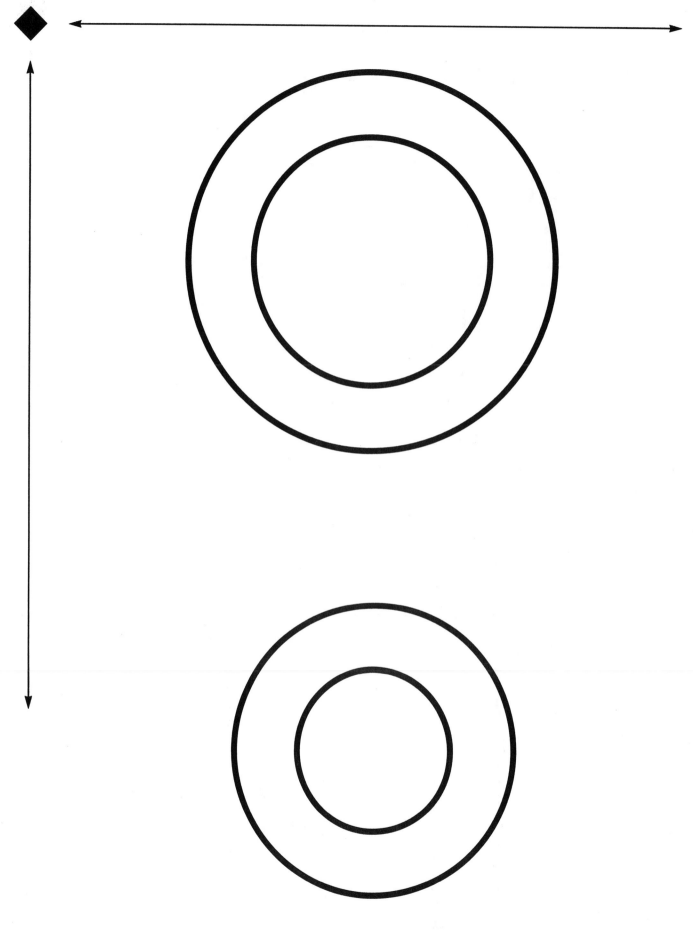

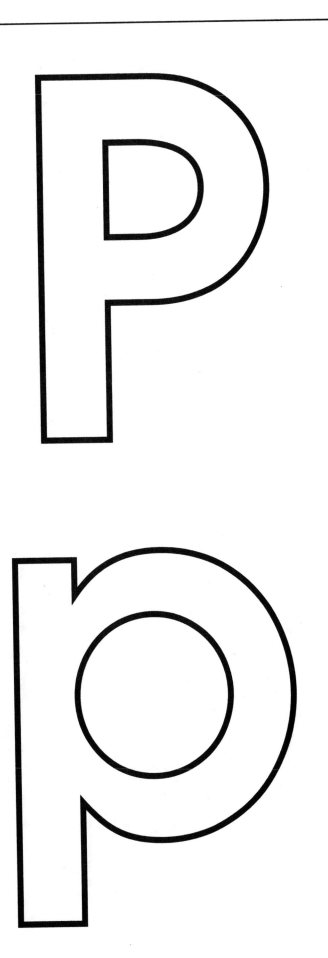

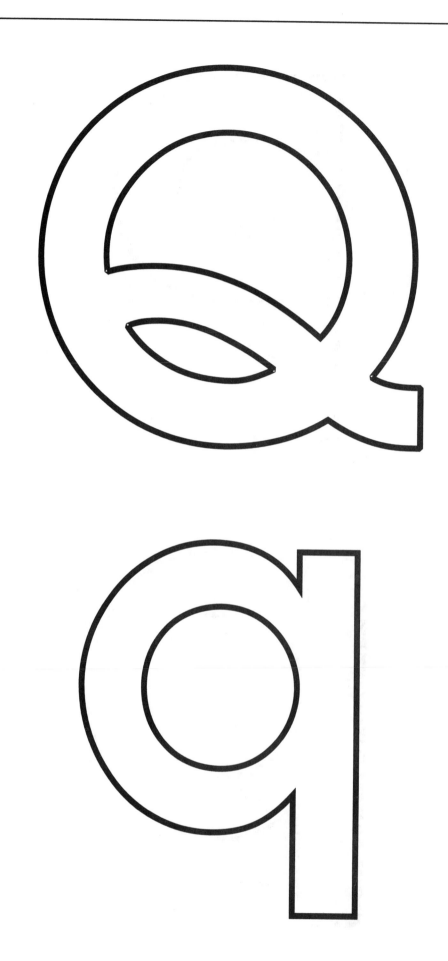

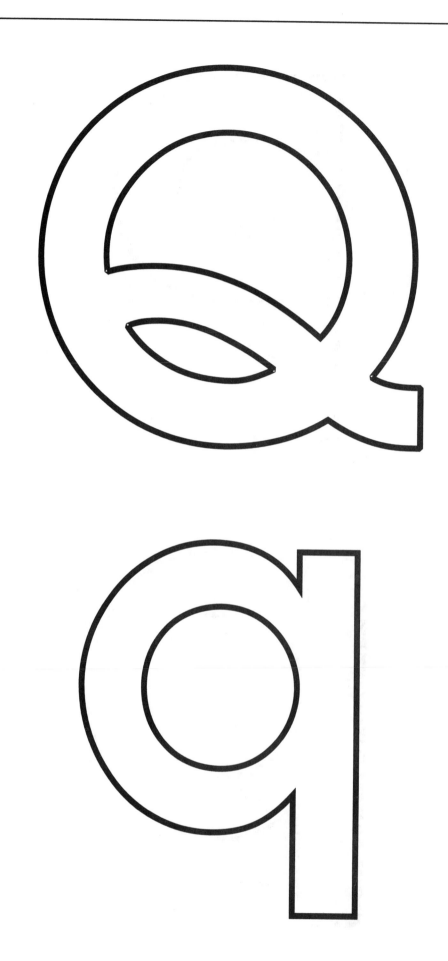

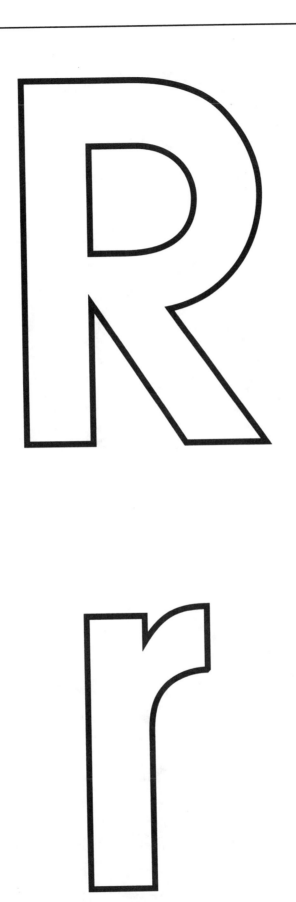

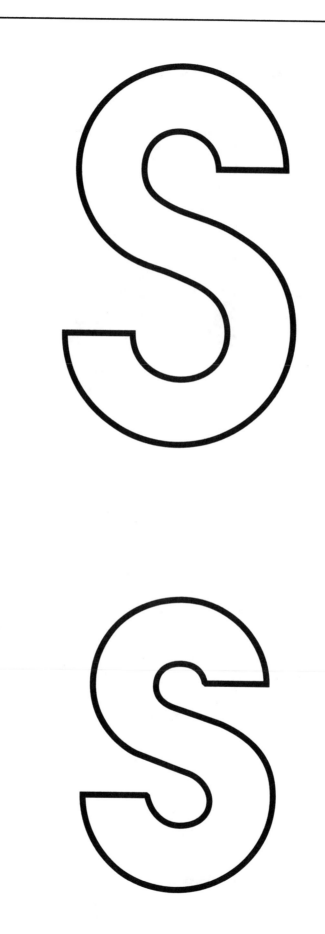

208

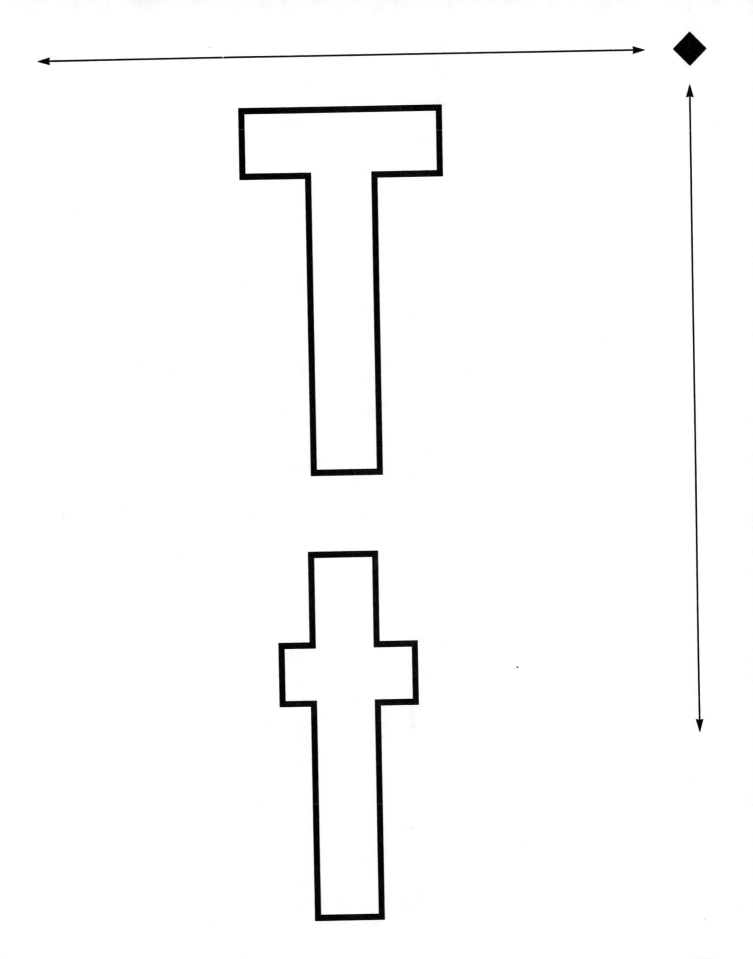

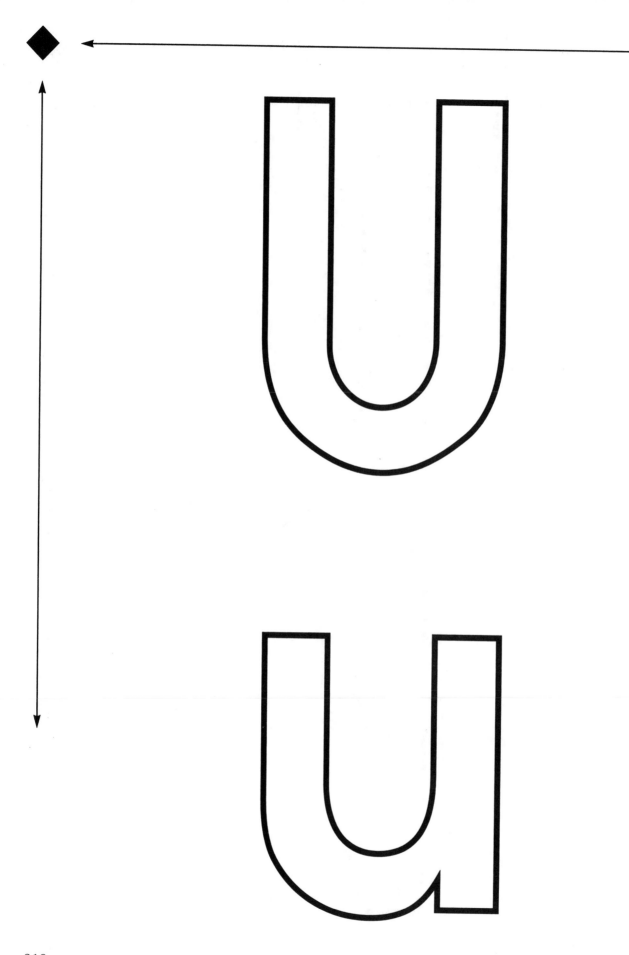

210

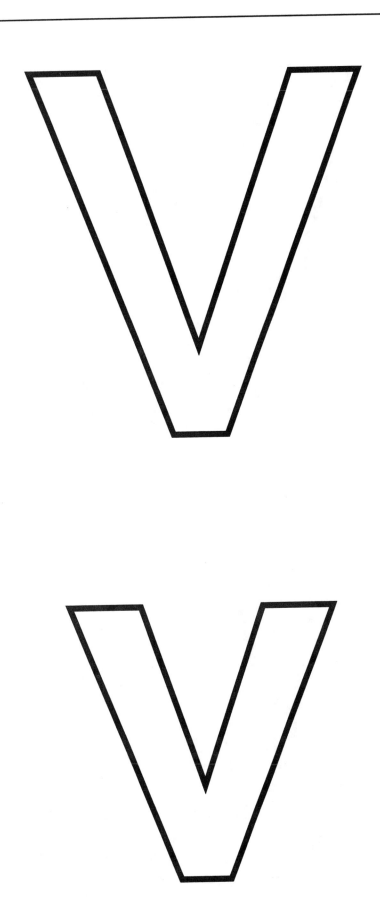

211

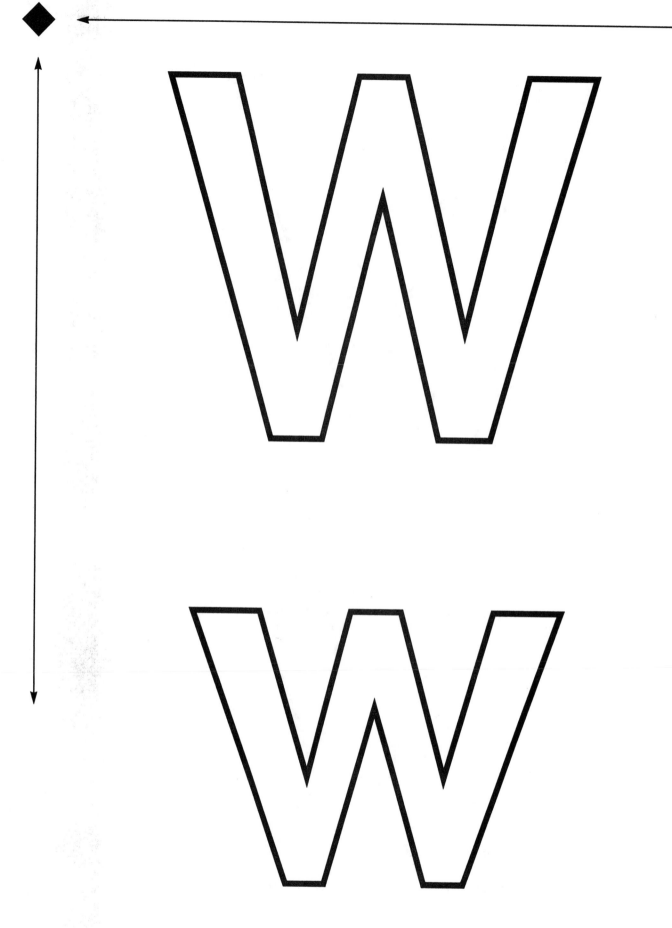

212

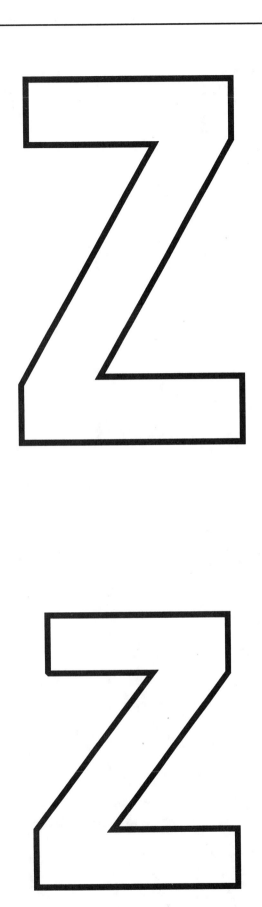

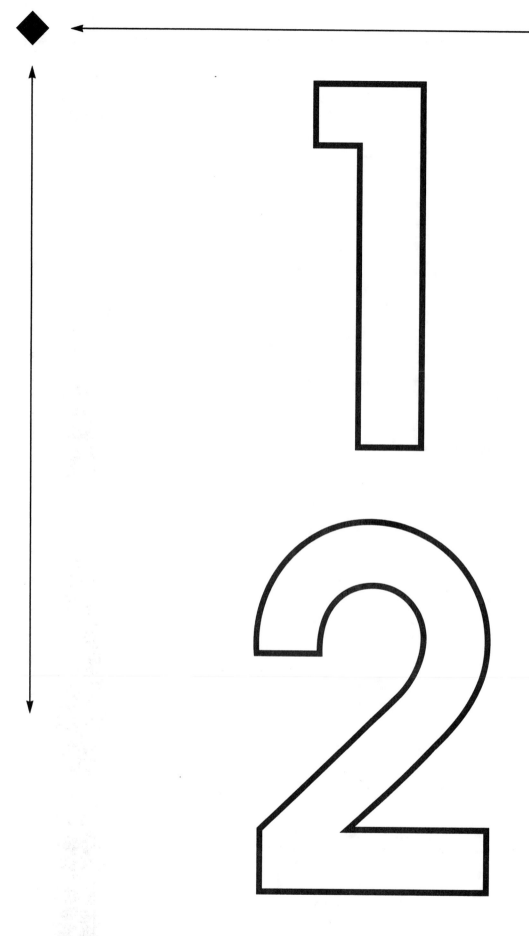

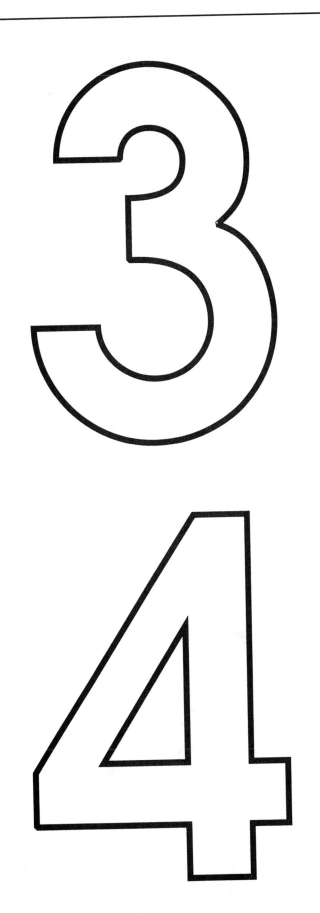

5

6

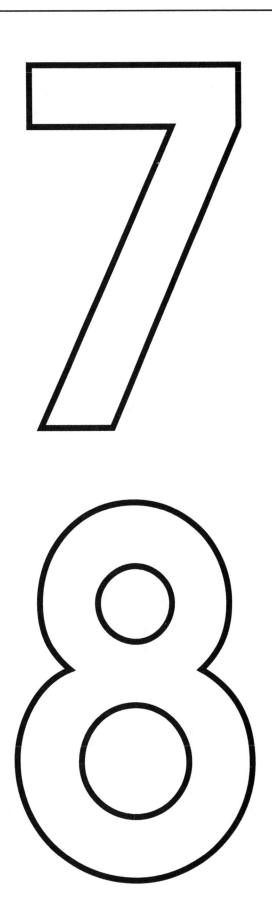

9

10

Theme Index

Terms Index